The Gardener's Book of
Herbs

Mary Page, NDH

FREDERICK WARNE

Published by Frederick Warne (Publishers) Ltd, London, 1984

Cover picture supplied by
Harry Smith Horticultural Photographic Collection

Material in this book, now fully revised and updated, originally
formed part of The Observer's Book of Herbs

ISBN Limp 0 7232 3235 0
ISBN Cased 0 7232 3236 9

Printed and bound in Great Britain by William Clowes Limited,
Beccles and London

Contents

Introduction

Although there is archaeological evidence that man was using plants at least 5000 years BC, the first comprehensive record of plants of herbal value was compiled in the fourth century BC by Hippocrates, the Greek physician known as the 'Father of Medicine'. He recorded many plants considered to be of medicinal value to mankind; a few of these are still listed in the *British Pharmacopoeia* today. In the first instance plants selected for their fragrance were used in religious ceremonies, and therefore only the priests of the various cults had the knowledge and experience to extend the use of plants to healing, and also to food and wine-making. Right up to the fifteenth century the gathering and cultivating of herbal plants was largely confined to the religious houses, these being the only centres of learning and havens of peace in a world of turmoil. The early manuscripts, the herbals, and later the stillroom books bear witness to the widening use our forebears made of these plants, and one is constantly amazed at their skill in selecting those of benefit to mankind, many of which are still in use in the present day.

By the nineteenth century this interest in herbs, at least for household use, appears largely to have waned, and there is little evidence of a widespread use of them in England. Many herbs for medicinal use, however, were imported from Europe and elsewhere, but during the two world wars of the twentieth century supplies were to a large extent cut off, and the collection and cultivation of herbs was revived in Great Britain with official encouragement. This led to a revival of interest among the general public. Herb farms and nurseries increased in size and importance and a growing number of enthusiasts began to use both culinary and medicinal herbs in the home. The tremendous upsurge in foreign travel in the second half of this century took the British public to the many Mediterranean countries in which herbs grow freely and have always been widely used to add interest to cuisines for which a generous supply of meat and imported foodstuffs are not readily available, as they were in Great Britain during her period of imperial expansion. In the present day the lavish amounts of expensive cuts of meat which were once taken for granted are often beyond the purse of the average household, and the modern housewife looks for ways of making the cheaper cuts appetizing and interesting. In this she is greatly helped by the many publications specializing in herbs and their uses in the kitchen. Also the mass production of food animals and the development of the techniques of food preservation by canning, drying and deep freezing can result in some loss of natural flavour, and this can be compensated for by the discriminating use of herbs.

Although all plants were once designated 'herbs', in modern usage the term may be taken to apply only to a special group of plants which contain many substances of great value to man in various ways, in medicine, in the manufacture of food and drink, perfumery and toilet preparations, and also for culinary and other uses in the home. Such plants are distinguished from vegetables in that they are used as additions to food and not as foods in themselves. Some of the substances do occur in vegetable plants, but in far less concentration. They are known as 'active principles' and can be divided into a number of groups, not all of which are found in any one family of plants. Little is known about their function in plants; some are thought to play a part in plant growth, others to be waste products of this. They may be found dispersed throughout the whole plant, or in greater concentration in certain parts, ie, in roots, stems, leaves, inflorescences or seeds.

Only a few herbs are grown commercially on a large scale in the British Isles today, and the British rely on imported herbs from worldwide sources. Many are still gathered in the wild in parts of Europe and Asia, where they grow in abundance and labour is cheap, but, as there are many strains and soil conditions are very variable, these wild herbs vary considerably in quality. Some herb plants have been bred for better growth and increased yields and are now cultivated on a commercial scale in these regions. In England in recent years the herb industry has expanded considerably. Numerous small herb farms are developing throughout the country and are raising pot plants for local sales. The larger firms are supplying fresh and dried herbs to the food industry for inclusion in processed foods, condiments and sauces. The most important area for this appears to be the Vale of Evesham, where mint, parsley, rosemary, sage and thyme are grown on a field scale.

This expanding interest in herbs and their uses is not confined to Great Britain; there is considerable evidence that a similar development is taking place in the United States and Canada, and also in New

6

Zealand and Australia. In the United States the practice of herbal lore can be traced back to the Pilgrim Fathers and other early settlers from Great Britain and Europe, who took their old herbals and a few herb plants with them to their new land. An interesting example of an early colonial herb garden can be seen in England at the American Museum at Claverton Manor on the outskirts of the city of Bath. In the nineteenth century the growing of herbs for medicine in America was largely in the hands of the Quakers and 81 hectares (200 acres) were cultivated by them in Massachusetts and around New York. Kay N. Sanecki in *The Complete Book of Herbs* (see page 141), published in 1974, refers to the present day expansion of herb farms in America, especially in California, and the developing trade in green-dried herbs was first promoted by an American commercial concern.

The pioneers who found new homes in Australia and New Zealand introduced a wealth of plants from Europe, including the many herbs which they had been accustomed to using in their former life. The interest in culinary herbs in both countries is being further stimulated as many Europeans continue to emigrate to the southern hemisphere, taking their particular cooking skills with them.

Herbs in the Garden

Aspect, Soil and Drainage

A large number of the culinary herbs were introduced into Britain by the Romans during their long occupation of northern Europe and by monks travelling to and from the Continent; most of these come from the Mediterranean regions and grow either on sun baked mountain slopes or in sheltered, well watered valleys. These factors govern their requirements in the garden. The woody plants, on the whole, are found where conditions are hot and dry, and therefore need to be planted in full sunshine on well drained, stony soil. These plants make relatively short growth each year and have means of protection from excessive water loss, such as hard textured leaves with reflexed margins and dense hairs on the undersides, eg, common thyme, or leaves entirely protected by a fine woolly covering, eg, sage. The herbaceous perennials, on the other hand, coming mainly from the valleys and water meadows, need a soil that is moderately fertile and moisture retaining, and shelter from strong winds and scorching sun. Some very useful herbs are annual or biennial and need similar conditions to these to encourage rapid growth and early seed development that will allow plenty of time for ripening. A thin soil and too free drainage for such plants will induce them to run to seed before they have made adequate growth, thus giving only a light seed crop. Only a very few herbs need shade for much of the day, eg, bergamot, a North American plant coming from a marshy habitat, and the ordinary garden mint, which if grown in sunny and dry conditions will become infested with rust.

Providing these requirements are met, the soil of the average garden is adequate for the culinary herbs. Shelter from wind is all important. Strong winds in spring will damage the young growth, and in summer will bruise the soft leaves of herbaceous plants, causing loss of essential oils. Sweet basil, with its large and very soft growth and tender leaves must be grown in the most sheltered area. Light sandy or chalky soils which tend to dry out in summer need an addition of humus in the form of well rotted farmyard manure, well decayed compost, or spent hops; this should be added when preparing such soils before planting. In nature humus accumulates in the dense mat of growth clothing the mountain slopes, but this does not occur in the more open planting under garden conditions, and on thin dry soils in hot summers herb plants make poor growth and their essential oils are less pleasantly aromatic. On the other hand, a tacky, heavy clay will also restrict growth, and the fleshy roots of certain herbaceous herb plants may rot in wet winters. Liberal applications of well decayed humus will make such soil friable, thus improving the drainage and encouraging strong root development. Manuring programmes for herbs are necessary only on commercial farms where high productivity is essential or where medicinal herbs are being grown for high yields of the required constituents. Then the normal fertilizing procedures are followed, ie, the addition of nitrogen when leaves are required, phosphates when plants are grown for flowers and seeds, and potash for harvesting roots. Thus feeding is related to the part of the plant required for the maximum yield of the drug it produces.

Planning

Many attractive plans of formal herb gardens are given in books and magazine articles on herb growing, often following the pattern of the Tudor 'knot' gardens with numerous small beds in geometrical designs, and these can be very decorative features in a garden. They are, however, quite unsuitable for the growing of a wide range of the useful culinary herbs, many of which are vigorous, tall and spreading plants that do not fit into the confined space of a formal plan. In large gardens with unlimited space such herb gardens can be laid out with beds in intricate patterns filled with the smaller herbs in the centre, and wide borders to accommodate the large spreading herbs surrounding them. An excellent example of this type of layout is the herb garden at Sissinghurst Castle, near Cranbrook in Kent, designed by the late Victoria Sackville-West and now in the care of the National Trust. It is often suggested that for the housewife's convenience a plot for growing herbs should be sited near the kitchen door, but such a position rarely fulfils all three of the necessary growing conditions outlined earlier and is often far too much shaded for the sun loving plants. Apart from the inconvenience of collecting, there is no reason why herb plants should not be dispersed throughout the flower garden, providing their growth requirements are met. A border planted with

Lemon Thyme   height 15 cm
(6 in) width 20–30 cm (8–
12 in)

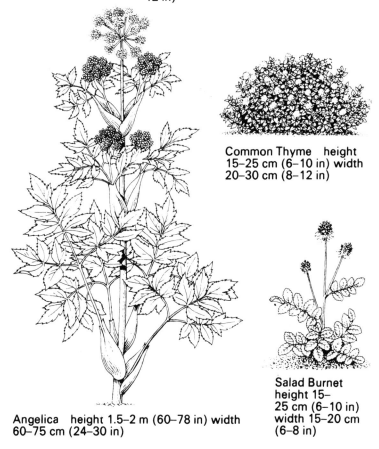

Common Thyme   height
15–25 cm (6–10 in) width
20–30 cm (8–12 in)

Salad Burnet
height 15–
25 cm (6–10 in)
width 15–20 cm
(6–8 in)

Angelica   height 1.5–2 m (60–78 in) width
60–75 cm (24–30 in)

Fig. 1   Growth patterns of various herbs

culinary herbs only will not be very colourful, as these plants tend to have small and insignificant flowers, but the planning of a garden should not be governed solely by the desire to provide flower colour. Plant form and height, and leaf shape and colour should always be taken into account, and in some gardens these features alone achieve an interesting and satisfying effect. A border planted ostensibly for culinary herbs could include a selection of some other herbs once considered to be of medicinal value but no longer important. These would provide a colourful display of flowers and make the border both showy and historically interesting. Any of the following would be suitable: camphor plant, comfrey, costmary (alecost), curry plant, delphinium, willow gentian, golden rod, orris root (*Iris florentina*), lady's mantle, madonna, tiger and turk's cap lilies, white marjoram, mullein, *Pyrethrum cinerariifolium*, sea holly, valerian, marigold.

A herb border should, if possible, face the prevailing sunlight and run east to west, and needs to be about 1·5 m (5 ft) wide, as it will be difficult to accommodate the taller plants in a narrower border. In anticipation of planting, a list of the herbs to be grown should be made, showing their relative heights when fully grown. A planting plan should then be drawn to scale on squared paper to indicate their position in the border. Obviously the tallest will occupy a position towards the back and the shortest towards the front or sunny edge, those of medium height being dispersed between them, but the placing must not be too rigidly adhered to or the final effect will be too regimented. Figs. 1–3 show the differing growth patterns of various herbs. The planting should not be done in straight lines, but an attempt made to achieve a random but orderly placing, with each individual plant interlocking with its neighbours, rather like a jigsaw puzzle. The space to allow around each plant depends on its spread; to a certain extent this can be taken to be two-thirds of its height when fully grown. Two examples of the layout for a herb garden can be seen on pages 146–147.

Remember when drawing up the plan to make contrasts between plant form and leaf shape and colour, and to allow spaces for the annual and biennial herbs which will be sown after the perennials have been planted. Probably only one plant of each of the very tall herbs such as angelica, fennel or lovage, or of spreading plants such as lemon balm or sweet cicely, will be needed for the average household, but the smaller herbs such as chives, marjoram and thyme should be planted in groups of three or five. Bushes such as lavender, rosemary and common sage will keep the border furnished during the winter months when

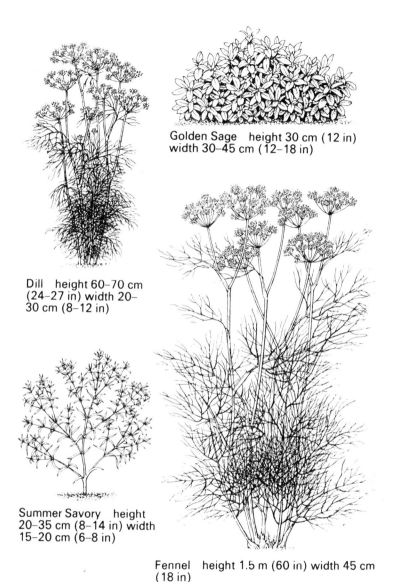

Golden Sage   height 30 cm (12 in) width 30–45 cm (12–18 in)

Dill   height 60–70 cm (24–27 in) width 20–30 cm (8–12 in)

Summer Savory   height 20–35 cm (8–14 in) width 15–20 cm (6–8 in)

Fennel   height 1.5 m (60 in) width 45 cm (18 in)

Fig. 2   Growth patterns of various herbs

13

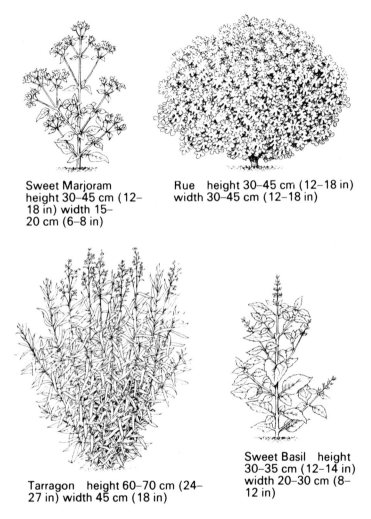

Sweet Marjoram
height 30–45 cm (12–
18 in) width 15–
20 cm (6–8 in)

Rue   height 30–45 cm (12–18 in)
width 30–45 cm (12–18 in)

Tarragon   height 60–70 cm (24–
27 in) width 45 cm (18 in)

Sweet Basil   height
30–35 cm (12–14 in)
width 20–30 cm (8–
12 in)

Fig. 3   Growth patterns of various herbs

most other things have died down, and, if space allows, a few shrubs with scented flowers such as allspice, damask roses, philadelphus or sweet briar could be fitted in at the back to give shelter and interest. In a garden where space is restricted it would obviously be possible to grow only a limited selection of the culinary herbs listed in the descriptive section of this book. The following will probably be found to be of most use in the kitchen: basil, chervil, chives, garlic, lovage, sweet marjoram, garden mint, parsley, rosemary, sage, summer savory, tarragon and thyme.

Preparation and Planting

The initial preparation of the herb border, to be carried out in autumn or winter, should consist of a thorough digging at least 20 cm (8 in) deep to encourage free rooting, and all roots of perennial weeds must be removed. A generous supply of compost should be added at the same time. Annual weeds, if numerous, can be controlled as soon as they begin to appear in spring by the use of a hoe. Chemical weed controls are not easy to apply on mixed borders containing herbaceous plants as they will be starting their new growth at different times; if such controls are used, great care must be taken to avoid damage to the young emerging shoots. As only a few plants of each perennial herb will be needed for a household, it is best to buy young plants in early spring for the initial planting. Most herbs can easily be raised from seed but there would be a delay of a year or more before the plants would produce any growth large enough for harvesting. For this reason seed sowing is usually restricted to annuals and biennials.

Maintenance

Once planted, a herb border, unlike a flower border, needs little attention apart from weeding, although after a period of three to four years any herbaceous plants which have become crowded with growth will need to be lifted, divided and replanted. This should be done in early spring, discarding all the weak central growth and using only the vigorous outside shoots in order to maintain a strong and healthy stock of plants. All woody plants should be examined from time to time and any long, straggling shoots cut back to buds developing nearer the roots. If no new growth is to be seen, however, do not attempt this cutting back, as bare wood rarely produces new shoots.

Yearly attention will be needed for the following herbs.

Early Spring   Bergamot.   Divide and replant each year for best results.

French majoram.   Trim last year's flowering shoots back to the new growth at the base.

Winter savory.   Cut back last year's wood to within 5 cm (2 in) of the ground.

Late Spring   Basil, sweet majoram, summer savory.   Sow seed in a frost-free place.

Hardy annuals and biennials.   Sow seed in the open garden in late spring.

Chives.   Begin cutting back plants in rotation and continue throughout the growing season.

Early Summer   Bergamot, lovage, tarragon.   If the ground is dry, water well and follow with a mulch of decayed compost.

Summer   Sage, thyme.   As soon as flowering has ceased cut back to within 5 cm (2 in) of the base of the new growth.

All herbaceous plants.   Cut out a few maturing shoots to encourage young growth.

Autumn   Chervil, parsley.   Sow seed for spring supplies.

Late Autumn   Garlic.   Plant cloves in the open garden in warmer regions; in cooler areas it is probably wiser not to plant until early spring.

Propagation

The majority of herb plants grow vigorously and present few problems in propagation. The average household will need only a few plants of any one herb, and propagating for the replacement of old plants can be carried out by one of the methods outlined below.

The culinary and household herbs can be grouped according to their habit of growth and placed in categories as follows.

Propagation by Heel Cuttings   *Shrubs* hyssop, lavender, rosemary, rue, sage, common thyme.

Short firm shoots of the current year's growth with a woody base and a heel of older wood are taken from the parent plant during the late summer. These are inserted into sandy soil in the open garden and

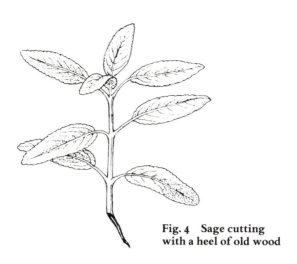

Fig. 4   Sage cutting with a heel of old wood

watered in. Further watering will be needed in dry weather. These cuttings will be well rooted by the following spring and can then be transferred to a permanent position.

Propagation by Division   *Subshrubs* common marjoram, French marjoram, variegated sage, winter savory, lemon thyme.

These are plants with woody roots but no definite leg, and propagation consists of lifting and breaking up the mat of roots into small pieces with the aid of two forks, or cutting with a sharp knife in the case of plants with very coarse roots. Lift the plant and thrust the forks into the centre, placing them back to back and gently levering them apart.

Fig. 5   Division of French marjoram

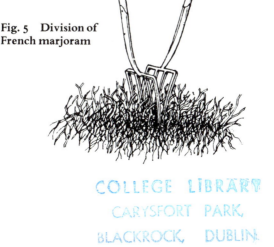

17

Some injury to the roots is bound to occur, and if the division is carried out in autumn the damaged roots may decay in the ensuing cold wet weather; in spring any injured tissue will heal rapidly as the warm weather encourages the new growth.

An alternative method is used when the growth is dense and twiggy. In spring the cushion of shoots is filled in the centre with sandy soil. Roots will form on the buried shoots during the summer and the plants can be pulled apart the following spring.

Fig. 6   Common thyme or variegated sage filled with sandy soil (for clarity, leaves are not shown)

Herbaceous plants chives, Roman chamomile, costmary, lemon balm, lovage, sorrel, tarragon.

These are lifted and divided as described for subshrubs as soon as new growth is seen in spring. All weak and crowded growth should be discarded and only the strong outer shoots saved for replanting.

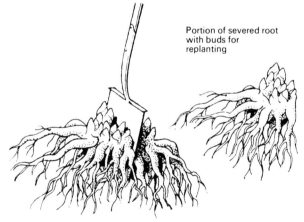

Portion of severed root with buds for replanting

Fig. 7   Fleshy root of lovage lifted and cut with a spade

Lovage and sorrel have fleshy roots and these will be lacerated if the division is carried out with forks. After lifting, the large mass of roots must be carefully split apart with a sharp spade or knife; some roots will need to be severed. Only roots with well formed buds should be replanted.

Tarragon grown on thin soils deteriorates rapidly and it may be unwise to lift and divide it. A serious check to the plant can be avoided by severing a shoot with roots from the parent plant, planting this in sandy soil and protecting it with a polythene bag supported by canes until it is certain that the young plant is well established. Because the soft tip will wilt it should be removed, as shown in Fig. 8.

Roman chamomile can be very easily propagated. On lifting it will be found that most shoots are well furnished with roots. These can be separated and treated as individual plants.

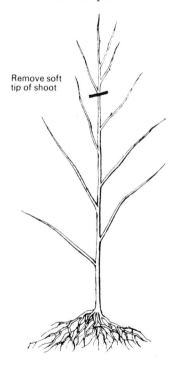

Remove soft
tip of shoot

**Fig. 8   Rooted shoot of tarragon severed
from the old plant during May**

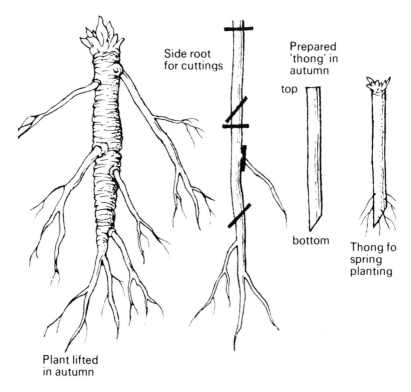

Side root
for cuttings

Prepared
'thong' in
autumn

top

bottom

Thong fo
spring
planting

Plant lifted
in autumn

Fig. 9   Horseradish root cuttings

Propagation by Root Cuttings   *Horseradish.* Plants with fleshy
roots which will form new buds are propagated by root cuttings.
When the crop of horseradish is harvested in autumn the side roots are
severed from the main roots, and root cuttings (thongs) are prepared
from the thickest of these by cutting them into 15 cm (6 in) lengths.
Straight cuts are made at the end nearest the crown and slanting cuts at
the lower end. These prepared cuttings are tied in bundles and stored
upright in moist sand for the winter months. During this time the cut
ends will callus and buds will form at the upper end. The following
spring they should be planted out with the upper end just below the
surface of the soil (see also p. 76).

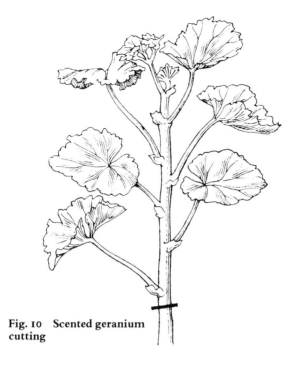

Fig. 10 Scented geranium cutting

Propagation by Half-ripe Cuttings *Scented geraniums.* These cuttings are prepared from shoots which have finished flowering by cutting with a sharp knife below the lowest leaf. The two bottom leaves are removed to produce a leg and any remaining flowers are removed. The cuttings are then inserted in sandy soil in pots, watered in, and kept in a shady spot until autumn, when they should be moved to a frost-free place for the winter.

Self-sown Seedlings *Angelica, borage, fennel, sweet cicely, common thyme.* These herbs seed freely and a few self-sown seedlings should be selected as replacements for the older plants when necessary.

List of Annual and Biennial Herbs *Hardy annuals* Anise, borage, chervil, coriander, dill, nasturtium, summer savory.

Half-hardy annuals Basil, sweet marjoram.

Biennials Caraway, parsley.

Herb Growing in Paved Gardens, Tubs and Window Boxes

With the spread of urban development and the consequent shortage and high cost of building land, present day gardens, especially in towns, may be so small that no ground can be spared for growing herbs or, in order to reduce maintenance to a minimum, the whole garden area may be paved, with only a few pockets of soil or the crevices between the paving stones available for planting. It would nevertheless still be possible to grow a worthwhile range of herbs, both decorative and useful, in such paved gardens, or in troughs, tubs or even window boxes.

A selection of herbs for planting in soil pockets between paving could be made from the following.

Sweet bay.   Although this is by nature a large shrub or tree it can be kept small by careful pruning. This is best done with secateurs rather than with shears to avoid damage to the leaves.

Lavender.   **1** Tall forms with a good scent, such as 'Grappenhall' and *Lavandula lanata* with broader silvery leaves.

2 Dwarf forms with a spreading habit but less scent: 'Hidcote', 'Munstead Dwarf', 'Twickle Purple'.

Rosemary.   There are several named forms that would be suitable: 'Tuscan Blue', 'Benenden Blue', 'Miss Jessup's Upright'.

Sage (*Salvia officinalis*).   The following forms have a low cushion-like habit and are useful where plants are needed to spread over the paving stones and give an air of informality: *S.o. icterina* with golden coloured foliage; *S.o. purpurea* with soft greyish-purple foliage; *S.o. tricolor* with grey-green foliage marbled with cream, gold, pink and purple.

In the crevices where there is likely to be considerable traffic, providing the drainage is satisfactory, low growing herbs will come to no harm when trodden on and will scent the air. Any of the following could be planted.

Salad burnet.

Roman chamomile.   The double form is the most decorative.

Wild or creeping thyme (*Thymus serpyllum*) in various colours. These can be used for culinary purposes. The variety 'Pink Chintz' is a particularly attractive little plant which makes a mound of hoary greyish foliage with an abundance of pink flowers.

Mentha requienii.   A tiny creeping mint with vivid green leaves and a strong peppermint aroma, suitable only for a shady, moist place.

Slightly taller herbs which would not stand being trodden on are: chives, hyssop, marjoram (common and French), winter savory, thymes.

All planting areas in paving must be well prepared by removing existing soil as deeply as possible and replacing it with a layer of broken brick, builders' rubble or stones for drainage. This should be covered with half decayed leaves or coarse compost, followed by a layer of good, well drained potting compost.

For troughs and tubs any of the shrubs suggested for paving would be suitable, or a selection of the smaller herbs mentioned, with the addition of eau-de-Cologne mint. A good range of these smaller herbs could be grown in the large tiered pots recommended for strawberries. Common mint and parsley could also be grown, but only if the container were placed in the shade.

Window boxes for both outside and inside the house can be filled with any of the shorter herb plants, remembering to include a few of the more attractive subjects such as salad burnet, hyssop, summer savory and the golden or silver thymes for a decorative effect. If bush basil, chervil, sweet marjoram or summer savory are required they should be raised from seed sown in small pots for planting in early summer.

The chosen containers must all be well drained. To facilitate free seepage from the drainage holes they should all be raised a little on narrow bricks or blocks of wood, and to prevent the soil washing out of the holes these must be covered, either with crocks, coarse stones, or pieces of perforated zinc which can be bought specially prepared for pot drainage from horticultural suppliers. These in turn should be covered with some coarse substance such as half decayed compost or finer stones to prevent silting, after which the containers should be filled to within 3 cm (1 in) of their rims with a good, well drained potting compost. Window boxes need to be firmly secured to the sill as they become very heavy when filled with soil.

The larger plants will need containers giving a minimum rooting depth of 30 cm (12 in), and for the smaller plants a minimum depth of 15 cm (6 in) should be allowed. With careful watering and occasional feeding with one of the proprietary pot plant fertilizers plants in large containers will only need renewing after five or six years' growth, but those in the shallower window boxes will need to be replaced each year to maintain satisfactory growth.

23

Herb Lawns

Certain low growing herbs will make a good dense turf which can be walked on without damage and will stand up well to dry or even drought conditions, but in normal circumstances they are to be recommended only for small areas, as they are planted rather than sown and this involves major problems of raising a large number of plants at one time and finding the extra labour for planting if the area is large. When the turf consists exclusively of herb plants it is generally sufficient to mow only two or three times in a season, as soon as the flowers appear, to keep the turf green and retain a smooth surface. The one exception to this is the creeping thyme, which is not mown until the flowers have faded. Where herbs and grass are mixed, however, weekly mowing throughout the season will obviously be necessary to keep the grass in check.

A fertile soil will not be satisfactory for a herb turf as it will encourage the growth of weeds and make the herbs too lush; therefore sand must be added to impoverish the soil, and this will also ensure the very good drainage required. In the first year a good deal of hand weeding will be necessary, but in subsequent years the growth will be so dense that the weeds will be suppressed. It is not possible to use selective weedkillers to check weeds in herb turfs as these will kill the herbs also.

There are three creeping herbs which are commonly used for making turfs.

Creeping thyme, *Thymus serpyllum*, obtainable with flowers in various shades of pink and purple, and also white.

Roman chamomile, *Chamaemelum nobile*, preferably either the double form or the flowerless form 'Treneague'. The double flowered chamomile is sturdier in growth than 'Treneague', which is only suitable for paths which will not be used a great deal, or for making the turf seats which were a feature of Tudor herb gardens.

Pennyroyal, *Mentha pulegium*, which makes a very close turf but needs a more fertile, moisture-retaining soil than the last two plants.

Herb lawns and paths are normally planted in spring, a stock of small plants having been accumulated during the previous year. Chamomile and pennyroyal are readily propagated by constantly dividing the stock plants and growing on the small rooted shoots in a nursery bed. Thyme is not so free-growing and will not respond to division so readily, so a larger number of stock plants will be required.

The prepared site is planted at 10–15 cm (4–6 in) intervals in spring, and by early autumn a good cover will have been achieved. If the summer is dry an occasional watering is advisable. Creeping thymes are usually planted in mixed colours: the plants remain in flower for several weeks and the effect is more attractive than with a single colour. Thyme 'carpets' can be made by planting in interlacing groups of colour to give the appearance of a tapestry. They are seen to best advantage if laid out on sloping ground, or in a bed slightly raised in the centre.

If a mixed herb and grass turf is required, Roman chamomile is the most suitable herb for the purpose. The grass must be established first and then the small chamomile plants can be inserted at 15–20 cm (6–8 in) intervals over the whole area in spring. Chamomile is exceptionally resistant to dry conditions and a mixed turf such as this does not show the effects of dry weather as much as a pure grass turf.

These herb lawns are a delightful addition to the garden, and when trodden underfoot give off a most refreshing fragrance, especially in the cool of the evening after a hot day.

Using Herbs

A definite line cannot be drawn between spices and culinary herbs. Both are of vegetable origin and a few can be included in both categories. Spices on the whole are obtained from plants growing in the tropics or sub-tropics and are used dried, and as they are very concentrated and strongly flavoured they are used only in very small amounts; thus their nutritional value is small. Herbs, often called 'sweet herbs', grow satisfactorily in any mild climate. The majority of the herbs described in the following pages of this book are cultivated throughout the temperate parts of the world. They can be used either fresh or dried. Herbs are added to food in greater quantity than spices, and if not used in excess are more delicate and subtle in flavour.

It is the essential oil in herbs which is of major importance. These oils deepen and enhance the flavours of food, and probably most people would consider this the reason for adding herbs to our diet, but they also contain vitamins, mineral salts (particularly potassium and calcium) and organic acids, and are actively beneficial to health. They promote the various bodily secretions, increase the circulation of the blood to the skin, improve the functioning of the kidneys, and by stimulating the flow of the gastric juices assist the digestive system. In the words of the sixteenth-century herbalist John Gerard, they 'promote a healthy desire for food'. In this age when so many people live in urban areas where freshly produced and unprocessed foods are virtually unobtainable, these sweet herbs can make a valuable contribution to the diet for the maintenance of robust health and vigour.

It is well known that condiments and spices can be damaging in certain health conditions, but few realize that they can be replaced to a large extent by herbs which are bland and non-irritant. A mixture of basil, marjoram, nasturtium, summer savory and thyme can be used fresh, dried, or in the form of a herb pepper to replace the true pepper, and if lovage is added the need for common salt is also reduced. Angelica, lemon balm and sweet cicely can be used to lessen the amount of sugar required to sweeten acid fruits such as black and red currants, gooseberries and rhubarb, and also to add a different flavour.

Many excellent cookery books have been published in recent years stressing the value of herbs and giving recipes for using them in great variety. Some recipes, however, may appear somewhat elaborate and time-consuming; it is a mistake not to use herbs to season the simple everyday dishes. Salt and pepper are added as a matter of course; the addition of one or two sprigs of fresh herbs or a spoonful of dried herbs should be equally automatic. Young leaves or the growing tips of herb plants contain the greatest amount of essential oil. This is released from the plant tissue by various means, by heating, chopping, bruising or pounding. The amount to be used will depend on personal taste, but it cannot be too strongly emphasised that herbs should never be added in such quantity that the natural flavour of the food is overpowered. As a general guide a dish for four persons will need 3–4 sprigs or a tablespoonful of chopped fresh herbs, but only a third of this amount of the more concentrated dried herbs. Which herbs to use with various foods is largely a matter of personal choice; variations can be made by making different selections. The classic *bouquet garni* called for in so many recipes is composed of 2–3 full length sprigs of parsley, 1 sprig of thyme and 1 bay leaf, sometimes with the addition of a sprig of marjoram. Parsley stems contain more flavour than the leaves; bay leaves are normally used whole, not chopped, as the flavour is very dominating. The herb mixture known as *fines herbes* consists of very finely chopped chervil, chives, parsley and tarragon. Chopped herbs or a *bouquet garni* are usually tied in a piece of muslin with a length of string for easy removal before serving.

Drying and Freezing Herbs

It is unlikely that valuable greenhouse or indoor space will be used for growing herbs throughout the winter; but they can be preserved for winter use during the summer by means of drying or deep freezing. Admittedly a wide range of dried herbs can be bought in most health food shops, and most of the supermarkets now stock them, but they will have been dried in bulk and this inevitably results in some loss of essential oil. Home dried herbs, if dealt with carefully, will in most cases be superior both in flavour and appearance, as well as being less costly.

The rules for the harvesting and preparation of herbs are the same for both drying or deep freezing. As bruising must be avoided, gathering is done with a sharp knife or pair of scissors, and the cut material should be placed in a flat basket or on a tray, never held in a bunch or heaped up in a deep container. Young leafy shoots only should be collected, just as the first flowers are about to open; at this stage the leaves contain the maximum amount of essential oils and other active principles. All growth harvested should be in perfect condition, any leaves that are old or wind damaged, or injured by insect or fungus attack being discarded. Harvesting should be done in the early morning before hot sun has evaporated the volatile oils. The herbs are likely to be dusty and soil splashed and will require washing. This is done by giving them a quick dip in cold water, after which they should be dried gently with a soft cloth. A colander or sieve is useful for washing small shoots such as marjoram or thyme. Drying or deep freezing must be done immediately after washing as the herbs will wilt if kept waiting, and therefore all the preparations should be made in advance.

Drying This needs to be done speedily, in order to retain the essential oils and preserve the green colour. Moderate heat, 35–38 C (95–100 F) is required, and this should be maintained throughout the drying process. If excessive heat is used the colour may be good but the aroma will be lessened. Free circulation of air must be allowed; if this is not available by natural means an electric fan may be used. Direct sunlight will spoil the colour and must be excluded. An airy loft can provide these conditions and at the same time supply plenty of free hanging space from the rafters; but any windows and doors must be covered, to cut out the light without impeding ventilation. The large herbs such as fennel, lovage, sage and tarragon should be tied in small bunches and hung up so that air can circulate round them; it is a good plan to re-bunch them at least once to ensure even drying. Small herbs such as marjoram, parsley and thyme are best spread out in thin layers on racks covered with curtain net. These can also be dried in the loft, or better still on the cooking stove after the cooking is finished, with the heat turned very low or even off; they may be placed in the oven with the door open, over a hotplate, or on the saucepan rack above the stove. An airing cupboard also makes a good place for drying these racks of small herbs, providing a good circulation of air can be maintained.

To dry juniper berries spread them on trays in a single layer and keep them at room temperature until slightly shrivelled. Then store in airtight jars.

Drying times vary considerably. Parsley will dry in a matter of hours but thick leaves may take two to three weeks. As soon as the leaves are crisp and break easily from the stem they should be rubbed into flakes, not powdered. Sifting through a colander will often help to remove small pieces of stem. The herbs should be stored in screw capped jars, preferably dark or paper covered, and kept in a dark place to preserve their colour as much as possible. They should never be stored in paper bags as these absorb the essential oil, nor in plastic bags which cause them to sweat and become musty. Bay leaves are not crumbled, but removed from the stems and left whole. The leaves of marjoram and thyme are removed from the woody stems once drying is finished, but the soft tips of stems and any immature flower buds may be included with the dried leaves.

Dried mixed herbs can be used in various assortments in any recipe calling for the addition of herbs. Alternatively, herb pepper or the even more pungent herb spice can be added directly to a dish, or placed on the dinner table for use as a condiment.

Mixed herbs
60 g (2 oz) parsley
30 g (1 oz) sweet marjoram
30 g (1 oz) winter savory
30 g (1 oz) black or lemon thyme
Mix well, bottle and label.

Herb pepper
15 g ($\frac{1}{2}$ oz) sweet marjoram ⎫
15 g ($\frac{1}{2}$ oz) rosemary   ⎬ powdered
15 g ($\frac{1}{2}$ oz) winter savory ⎪
15 g ($\frac{1}{2}$ oz) thyme   ⎭
15 g ($\frac{1}{2}$ oz) powdered mace
15 g ($\frac{1}{2}$ oz) freshly ground black pepper
Mix herbs and spices. Then sift, bottle and label.

Herb spice
30 g (1 oz) basil   ⎫
30 g (1 oz) bay leaves   ⎬ powdered
30 g (1 oz) sweet marjoram ⎪
30 g (1 oz) thyme   ⎭
1 rounded tablespoon black pepper
1 rounded tablespoon powdered cloves
1 rounded tablespoon powdered mace
1 rounded tablespoon powdered nutmeg
Mix herbs and spices. Then sift, bottle and label.

Freezing Preserving herbs for winter use by deep freezing retains both the natural green colour and all the essential oil. Opinions vary on the necessity of blanching, but, as with vegetables, blanching is advisable if the herbs are to be stored for any length of time, in order to avoid the deterioration of colour and flavour due to the action of enzymes. To blanch plunge the soft leafy shoots into boiling water for one minute, then cool in ice cold or running water and freeze immediately. Small bunches of herbs, either singly or made up into *bouquets garnis*, sufficient for one dish, should be placed separately on the freezing tray; once frozen they can be packed into containers. The containers should be rigid if possible, as frozen herbs are extremely brittle, and they must be airtight to prevent the strong aroma of the herbs from escaping and permeating other foods. For economy of time a single bunch of the appropriate herb can be included in each packet of vegetables to be frozen, eg, mint with green peas or summer savory with beans.

Herbs can also be chopped and packed into the sections of ice cube trays, which are then filled with water and frozen. The cubes can then be removed and stored in boxes for use as required. Chopped herbs can also be packed in small envelopes of freezer foil, then sealed and frozen. All packages of herbs should be clearly labelled before being frozen.

It is now possible in some areas to purchase frozen herbs from retailers stocking deep frozen foods.

Herb vinegars Herb-flavoured vinegars are used to give variety to salad dressings, sauces and mustards. The selected herb is washed and lightly bruised and then steeped in wine or cider vinegar in a closed glass or earthenware container for a period of two to six weeks. The vinegar is then strained through muslin and bottled for use.

Garlic vinegar Crush eight cloves of garlic with a sprinkling of salt, cover with one pint of boiling vinegar and leave for two weeks. Then strain off the liquid and bottle.

Mint vinegar Fill a wide-necked jar with lightly packed sprigs and cover with vinegar. Strain after two weeks and bottle.

Tarragon vinegar Fill a wide-necked jar with freshly picked leaves and add vinegar to cover. Leave in a cool place for about six weeks. Then strain, adding more vinegar if the flavour is too strong, and bottle. Other herbs such as basil, marjoram and thyme may be used in the same way.

In the list of further reading (p. 141) those books marked (C) contain detailed recipes using a wide range of herbs.

Description of Species

A note on the use of names in text and index: family names are printed in capitals, eg, COMPOSITAE, species names in italics, eg, *Matricaria recutita*, common names in Roman type, eg, Colt's-foot. Varietal names appear in quotation marks, eg, 'Hidcote'.

Agrimony

Agrimonia eupatorium L.
Family ROSACEAE

This is a plant which is widespread throughout the northern hemisphere except for the arctic regions. It is seen in hedgerows, on roadsides and on wastelands. One of its common names, church steeples, refers to the sharp pointed spikes of yellow flowers. The erect stems, 30–60 cm (12–24 in) tall, bear distinctive pinnate leaves about 15 cm (6 in) long. These are divided into pairs of coarsely toothed leaflets 3–4 cm (1¼ in) long, and between each pair there are 2–3 pairs of smaller leaflets. Both stems and leaves are clothed with soft hairs. The long terminal spikes carry many small five-petalled yellow flowers, each with a small tri-cleft leafy bract. As the seed ripens the grooved receptacle, covered with many hooked spines, enlarges and becomes woody, forming a reddish-brown burr about 1 cm (⅓ in) in diameter. These small ripe fruits attach themselves to anything that brushes against them, and this accounts for the old country names of cockle burr and stickwort.

Agrimony is not to be confused with hemp agrimony, *Eupatorium cannabinum*, a member of the Compositae family. This is a very different plant only to be found on moist soils, very often in wet ditches.

Uses In earlier times agrimony was very widely used as a healing herb. The ancient Greeks valued it in the treatment of cataract of the eyes, and infusions of it were used as a cure for sore throats and chronic catarrh, and for diarrhoea in children. The leaves and seed were also put into wine. In the present day the leaves and flowering spikes are gathered in the wild, before the seed is formed, and the drug obtained after drying is used as a constituent of medicine for improving the function of the digestive organs and for a general tonic. It is also used externally in preparations for treating inflamed gums and for promoting the healing of skin troubles and minor wounds.

The whole plant yields a good yellow dye which is used by those who are interested in home dyeing, and it is also grown commercially for this purpose for the textile industry.

Garden Angelica

This handsome plant is often grown for its architectural appearance in the garden as well as its value as a herb. It grows approximately 150 cm (5 ft) tall with erect, smooth, stout stems and deeply indented fan-like leaves. These may be 75 cm (3 ft) wide with succulent petioles and tend to spread horizontally; the whole plant is a fresh light green. The small whitish or greenish-yellow flowers appear from mid June on branching stems carrying heads of compound globular umbels. The whole plant when bruised gives off a delightfully refreshing aroma. It is a native of Northern Europe and Russian Asia, but is not found in the wild in Great Britain except as a garden escape.

A somewhat similar plant, *A. sylvestris*, commonly known as wild angelica, has a wider distribution in the northern hemisphere, including marshy regions in Britain. This is a taller plant with more slender stems flushed with purple and slightly downy; the flowers are pinkish white and the whole plant has little or no flavour.

A. archangelica was greatly revered in the Middle Ages throughout Europe; it was considered to be an antidote for many ills, especially the plague. It was also used in rituals against the power of witches, and for this reason its common name was the root or the herb of the Holy Ghost. When it was introduced into the milder climate of southern Europe its flowering coincided with one of the feast days of St Michael. This accounts for the specific name 'archangelica'.

Angelica archangelica L.
Family UMBELLIFERAE

Cultivation   *A. archangelica* is a short-lived plant, dying back to ground level each year. It may not flower and seed for two or three years, but once seed has formed the plant will die. However, if the flower heads are removed before the seed is set the life of the plant can be prolonged for a further one or two years. The usual practice is to allow some of the seed to fall to the ground and germinate naturally, because seed harvested and kept for later sowing is often unsuccessful. In the following spring thin out and transplant the seedlings. *A. archangelica* must be grown in moist soil in a position where it will be in shade during the hottest part of the day. In full sun the growth will be poor and the leaf stems tough and stringy. Plenty of room is needed for the wide spreading leaves.

Culinary Use   Chopped young leaves may be added to salads, and fresh leaf stems may be cooked with acid fruits such as blackcurrants, gooseberries and rhubarb to counteract tartness, using 60 g (2 oz) of angelica to 500 g (1 lb) of fruit. Its flavour is mild and sweet, but quite distinctive. Candied angelica (commercially exported mainly from France) can be prepared in the home from the young, fleshy leaf stems, although the process is somewhat lengthy. The selected stems are cut into 10 cm (4 in) lengths and steeped in cold salted water – 8 g to 1 litre of water ($\frac{1}{4}$ oz to $1\frac{3}{4}$ pt) – for ten minutes to retain the green colour, then rinsed well and boiled gently until tender. The outer skin and any stringy fibres should then be removed, and the pieces candied by the normal candying process. In addition to its conventional use for decorating cakes and desserts, candied angelica adds a delicious flavour to pie fillings and preserves.

Other Uses   A refreshing tonic tea can be made from the fresh leaves, using a handful of crushed leaves to a litre of water with honey and lemon to taste. The essential oil which is obtained from the dried roots, leaf stems and seed is used in medicine for the treatment of gastric disorders. It is an ingredient of many forms of 'alternative medicine', eg, as in cures for coughs and colds, tonics for improving the appetite and herbal tea to aid digestion. Flatulence may be relieved by chewing raw stems. The oil is also used in the processing of food and for flavouring gin and chartreuse.

Anise

Owing to the short growing season this sun loving annual is seldom grown in the British Isles although it is very decorative. A long season of growth is necessary for the production of seed. It grows 60 cm (25 in) high and has erect, slender, branched stems. The delicate green foliage, as in so many plants of this family, is varied on the one plant; its lower leaves are coarsely toothed with long petioles, and the others deeply cut with short petioles. Flowering does not begin until late summer, when an abundance of loose umbels of small whitish flowers appears on the upper stems, these being followed by aromatic, oval-shaped, brown-ribbed fruits.

Cultivation   Anise will only grow well on poor dry soils in sunny areas. The seed is generally sown direct in mid spring. To increase the length of the growing season the soil can be warmed by covering it with cloches 10–14 days before sowing and leaving these on to speed up growth. Alternatively, a pinch of seed can be sown in several pots and germinated inside. In this case reduce the seedlings to one per pot when about 3 cm (1 in) high, finally planting these in open ground about 20 cm (8 in) apart without disturbing the roots, when all danger of frost has passed. The seedlings sown outside will need to be thinned

Pimpinella anisum L.
Family UMBELLIFERAE

when large enough to handle. In both cases the protection given in the early stages should encourage early fruiting. As soon as the fruits turn yellow the plants should be cut, tied in small bunches, and hung upside down in a warm airy place to finish ripening. A cloth should be placed below to catch the falling seed. When fully ripe the seeds can be separated by rubbing them from the branches.

Culinary Use Anise has a liquorice flavour. The plant is grown mainly for seed production, but as with many other herbs the leaves may be added to salads or used as a garnish. The seeds may be cooked with beetroot, cabbage and carrots, and put into bread, biscuits and cakes or sprinkled over them before cooking, as is done with sesame seeds. They also add a pleasant flavour to drinks and puddings.

Other Uses The essential oil is used in perfumery, for cough lozenges, in the food processing industry and in the manufacture of the liqueur anisette.

This oil (*oleum anisum*) is also obtained from a woody shrub indigenous to SE Asia, *Illicium anisatum*, a plant with small creamy white flowers commonly called star anise as the ripe carpels form a many-pointed star. This shrub can be grown in southern England in sheltered woodlands on lime free soils.

Sweet Basil
Bush Basil

The basils must be treated as half hardy annuals in temperate climates. Sweet basil is indigenous to southern Asia and the Middle East and is grown extensively in the sub-tropics where it is widely used for flavouring. Bush basil is a native of South America; it is less aromatic and less generally cultivated. Sweet basil is a branching, bushy plant growing 30 cm (1 ft) or more high, with broadly ovate leaves 8 × 4 cm (3 × 1½ in) which are remarkably cool and soft to the touch. The shoots terminate in spikes carrying whorls of whitish flowers, often flushed with purple, with conspicuous leafy calyces and bracts. There are several forms in cultivation; one is 'lettuce leaved' and another deep purple and considered very attractive. Bush basil grows only 15 cm (6 in) high and the numerous short stems are clothed with small narrow leaves. It is easier to grow and less liable to wind damage than sweet basil, but is less fragrant. In both species the flower spikes are far more aromatic than the leaves; this is very evident after drying.

Ocimum basilicum L.
Ocimum minimum L.
Family LABIATAE

Sweet Basil

Cultivation   Basil is not an easy plant to maintain in good condition. Its growth is very tender and easily damaged by careless handling or exposure to wind, and it must be grown in a sheltered position where it will be protected from scorching sun. Bush basil, however, will tolerate adverse conditions better than sweet basil. The seed should be sown in a frost-free place in spring, and as root disturbance causes a check to growth it is usual to sow a few seeds in small pots to avoid having to prick out. Thin the seedlings and pot on as necessary, and finally, when all danger of frost has passed, plant them in the open without any root disturbance, into well drained soil with plenty of humus. In dry weather water freely. The highly aromatic flower spikes as well as single leaves should be gathered, and continuous picking of these will encourage the bushy habit of the plant which is desirable. At all times bruising of the foliage should be avoided.

It is possible to maintain a winter supply of basil by growing either plant in containers on a window-sill in a warm room.

Culinary Use   All the experts agree that basil is one of the most important herbs in the kitchen. It has a rich and subtle flavour and is used on its own, rather than mixed with other herbs, with cooked and raw foods, either freshly chopped or pounded, or in the dried form. To preserve the aroma it is best to add it in the last few moments of cooking or just before serving. It is considered an essential herb in Italian cookery, and is particularly delicious with any dish containing tomatoes, especially raw tomato salads. It is used with roast meats, poultry, pasta, cheese dishes and omelettes, soups and sauces, and greatly enhances the flavour of any food with which it is used.

Other Uses   Basil is used in herbal remedies for digestive disorders; and a tonic may be made by steeping it in wine. The dried herb can be pulverized and made into a medicinal snuff, and this is recommended as a cure for headaches.

Oil of basil is used in the perfumery industry and also as a flavouring for processed foods.

Sweet Bay

An evergreen tree native to the Mediterranean regions growing 10–15 m (35–40 ft) high. This is an upright tree with many branches and numerous shoots clothed with dark green leathery ovate leaves with

Laurus nobilis L.
Family LAURACEAE

well defined margins, up to 10 × 4 cm (4 × 1½ in) long, with pale
yellowish green undersides and short reddish leaf stalks. In English
gardens bay is often seen growing as a dense bush and is also sold by
nurserymen as a decorative standard in a tub. When the leaves are held
up to the light a fine network of veins will be seen; these contain the
essential oil and when crushed give off a strong aroma. The small
flowers appear in spring in groups of four to six as fluffy greenish
yellow balls in the leaf axils. The fruits are oval and dark green,
becoming blackish purple when ripe, but these are rarely seen in
northern Europe.

Sweet bay is also known as bay laurel, but various other plants also
called 'laurel' should not be confused with it. One in particular, the
cherry laurel, *Prunus laurocerasus*, is poisonous, but it differs greatly in
appearance from sweet bay as its leaves are large, oblong and a lighter
green, and lack the attractive aroma.

Cultivation Shelter from cold winds is essential for this tree, coming
as it does from the warm climate of southern Europe. It grows best in
full sunshine and on a well drained soil. In a small garden, however, it
can be grown successfully as a shrub by restricting its roots and keeping
the shoots trimmed back, but as it is very slow growing some years
will elapse before it will have made sufficient growth to allow leaves
to be gathered for use in the kitchen. It can also be grown in a tub, and

this is definitely advisable in cooler regions so that it can be moved into a cold greenhouse for the winter, as the leaves may be badly damaged by severe weather. Propagation is by half-ripe cuttings, preferably with the use of a rooting substance. The cuttings can be inserted in sandy soil in a frame in late summer, or in a sheltered place in the open. The proportion of cuttings which root is generally low, and subsequent growth is slow for the first five to six years; but once established the growth of the young plant will be satisfactory.

Propagation can also be carried out by layering in late summer if there is a branch near to the soil. A sliver of wood should be raised from ripened growth at the base of a young shoot; the branch should then be anchored firmly to the soil and the cut covered with a sandy mixture. In twelve months' time, if rooting has taken place, sever the shoot between the tree and the wound to form a new plant.

Culinary Use A bay leaf is a component of a *bouquet garni*, and bay leaves, either fresh or dried, have many uses in cookery, in marinades, sauces, casseroles and soups, with boiled beef or ham, soused fish and many vegetables, especially Jerusalem artichokes, aubergines and carrots. They also impart a sweet, delicate flavour to custards and milk puddings and other milk-based dishes. As the essential oil is strong, the leaves are rarely chopped or pounded but used whole or just cracked in one or two places to release the oil. One leaf is sufficient in a *bouquet garni* and one or two in a pint-sized dish for a milk pudding.

Herbal Use The oil obtained from leaves and berries of sweet bay is used in herbal remedies for rheumatic complaints.

Bearberry

This evergeen prostrate shrub grows freely in the cooler regions of the northern hemisphere. It is found only on the porous acid soils where there is a large accumulation of plant debris, such as moorlands and open carboniferous woodlands. Large colonies are often seen spreading over the cool northern slopes of mountains, where humus has collected amongst the crevices and boulders. The slender wiry stems make close carpets or hummocks. The small, leathery yet glossy leaves 2·5 × 1 cm (1 × $\frac{1}{3}$ in) are oblong and taper to the base; the terminal clusters of small urn-shaped flowers are usually white but may be tinged with red, and are followed by bright red berries.

Arctostaphylos uva-ursi L.
Family ERICACEAE

Cultivation This creeping shrub with its shining evergreen leaves is an attractive ground cover plant for the front of a border on lime free soils. Plenty of decayed leaf mould or peat should be worked into the surface layer of the bed, and the bearberry should be planted in partial shade, and watered freely in periods of drought. The plant can be increased very easily by carefully detaching rooted stems from the parent plant; frequent disturbance of the whole plant should be avoided. It flowers in spring and early summer, and in autumn the glossy scarlet fruits are an added attraction.

Uses Bearberry contains compounds used in pharmacy for the treatment of urinary disorders, and is also a useful internal disinfectant and an aid to the cure of digestive troubles, but it should only be used under medical supervision as excessive use can have harmful consequences.

The drug is obtained from the small evergreen leaves, which are collected throughout the summer and autumn, the main source of supply being northern Europe. Drying must be done with care to avoid fermentation, which would result in its useful components being lost.

Monarda didyma L.
Family LABIATAE

Another name for sweet bergamot is North American swamp plant, and this is indicative of the conditions it requires. The genus *Monarda* is found in marshy regions of North America, and this species, *M. didyma*, grows mainly in the swampy areas surrounding Lake Michigan and Lake Ontario. Only the true *M. didyma* is really fragrant, and therefore it is the only species that should be included in the herb garden. This plant has bright scarlet flowers and showy red bracts carried on erect leafy stems about 50 cm (1½ ft) high. These stems, like those of other plants in the Labiatae family, are quadrangular, with opposite leaves which are olive green and slightly velvety. The scarlet flowers are in dense axillary and terminal whorls and are interspersed with the conspicuous red bracts, giving the plant a very striking appearance. A far less fragrant species, *M. fistulosa* L., taller and with purplish mauve flowers, has been hybridized with *M. didyma*, producing a range of plants with flowers of varying shades from pink to purple. These are all useful plants, but for the flower garden only.

Sweet bergamot should not be confused with bergamot mint, *Mentha* x *piperata* var. *citrata*, which is the mint more generally known as eau de cologne mint.

Cultivation A moisture retaining soil is required, and this should be loose and open in texture and preferably lime free. Plenty of humus should be worked into the surface before planting. A shady situation is necessary unless frequent watering can be given. For vigorous growth frequent replanting is essential, so that the soil can be reconditioned for this shallow rooted plant with its abundance of surface rooting runners. Careful handling is necessary. In many gardens *M. didyma* tends to die out in winter, especially on soils which become compacted by heavy rain, and as a precaution, as soon as the summer shoots have died, it is wise to over-winter some of the carpeting overground runners in light leafy soil in an airy cold frame. Propagation is most commonly carried out by potting up small pieces of the rooted runners into sandy, leafy soil, taking care not to damage the somewhat fragile growth. Alternatively, plants can be raised from seed, but this is a slower method producing far more plants than are needed in one garden.

Culinary Use Young bergamot leaves have a delicate spicy flavour which is particularly appreciated with pork; they can be placed whole on a roasting joint or chops before cooking, or used to flavour a gravy or sauce. They can also be chopped and added to green salads, and shredded flowers can be used in the same way and will add colour as well as flavour. Dried leaves and flowers make a soothing drink when infused, or a small quantity can be added to a pot of Indian tea and will give it a subtle extra flavour. Oswego tea made from the leaves and flowers of the bergamots is so called from the tribe of Red Indians who inhabited the swamplands surrounding the Oswego River on the southeastern side of Lake Ontario, where the plants grew in abundance. During the troubles in America which led to the 'Boston Tea Party' in 1773, in protest against the imposition of a tax on tea by the British government, Oswego tea was used as a substitute for imported tea in many American households.

The fragrant orange-scented oil known as essence of bergamot is obtained from the peel of the bergamot orange, *Citrus Bergamia*, and used in the perfumery industry. This orange is a small tree with white fragrant flowers followed by pear-shaped fruits about 7 cm (3 in) in diameter which are pale yellow and thin-skinned. It is grown only in southern Calabria, but takes its name from the town of Bergamo in Lombardy.

Borage

Borago officinalis L.
Family BORAGINACEAE

This is a quick growing annual related to the forget-me-nots and similar to them in that it is very free seeding. It is native to the Mediterranean regions and will be found growing freely on light soils throughout the temperate world. It is a bulky plant with succulent branching stems which may grow 60 cm (24 in) or more high. The numerous dull olive green leaves, broad at the base and tapering to a point, may be 25 cm (10 in) long at ground level, becoming progressively smaller near the much branched flowering stems. Stiff whitish hairs are distributed over the whole plant, distorting the leaf surfaces and making them rough to handle. The branching shoots terminate in scorpioid racemes of attractive, vivid blue, five-petalled flowers about 3 cm (1 in) in diameter. The petals are slightly reflexed, exposing the conspicuous cone of five black anthers. The seeds are large, black and three-sided.

Cultivation The seed is normally sown where the plants are to grow, but they can be transplanted if this is more convenient. Seedlings are thinned or transplanted 30 cm (1 ft) apart. The plants grow quickly, and often two or three generations can come from one spring sowing or from self-sown seeds in one year on light soils. The last seedlings to germinate will over-winter and provide plants which flower early the following spring. These plants and those from an early spring sowing may grow so rapidly that by midsummer they will probably become top-heavy and ungainly with too great a profusion of flowering shoots. By this time much seed will have been scattered in the vicinity, so that the large old plants may be discarded and young plants grown on in their place. On heavy soils, however, seedlings are unlikely to survive the winter and some seed must be harvested each autumn and stored for sowing the following spring. On light soils this delightful plant, if not kept in check, may prove to be too invasive and unwanted seedlings will appear everywhere in the garden.

Culinary Use   Borage contains nitrate of potassium, calcium and a saline constituent, which are said to be valuable in salt-free diets. The leaves can be cooked with cabbage and spinach, and in soups, and very young leaves and tips of growth added to salads. Leaves and flowers are put into wine and cider cups, and like cucumber have a cooling effect. The flowers can be crystallized and used for cake decoration.

Other Uses   Borage plants are collected and dried for the value of their mucilage, saponin and tannin content, and are used mainly as herbal infusions for the treatment of kidney and bladder disorders and rheumatism.

Caraway

This biennial plant is native to central Europe and countries bordering the Mediterranean; it is now widely dispersed and has become a common weed of waste land, particularly in regions where it is grown as a commercial crop. It grows 40–60 cm ($1\frac{1}{2}$–2 ft) tall, with a root system and life cycle similar to that of a carrot. The fleshy root is formed in the first year, with a rosette of feathery foliage. In the second year the slender erect stems with smaller foliage branch freely into flat umbels of small white flowers. These are followed by light brown strongly ribbed fruits.

Carum carvi L.
Family UMBELLIFERAE

Cultivation   Caraway requires a well drained, friable soil and an open, sunny position. The seed is sown in early summer in the position where the plants are to grow and the seedlings are thinned out to 10 cm (4 in) apart as soon as they are large enough to handle. The plants will flower the next year in early summer, and the fruits will begin to ripen about 8 weeks later. When the main umbels are ripe the plants should be cut to the ground, tied in small bunches, and hung up in an airy shed over a cloth to catch the seed. This is then dried thoroughly before being stored in an airtight container.

Culinary Use   Caraway seed has a very distinctive spicy flavour and is added to rye bread, cakes, meat and fish dishes, beetroot and potatoes. It is excellent cooked with cabbage, and is also used in certain cheeses and pickles. If surplus plants are grown, some roots may be dug in the first year and cooked as a vegetable. Young foliage may be chopped for use with a green salad.

Other Uses   The aromatic essential oil from caraway seed is used in the food industry and in the preparation of the liqueur kümmel. Like many other herbs, caraway was held in far greater esteem in the eighteenth century. Roasted apples with caraway comfits were served after a rich heavy meal to ward off indigestion, and it was believed to prevent constipation and keep gout at bay.

Caraway is widely grown on a commercial scale in the Netherlands and Germany, both for seed and for the oil obtained from it. The drug extracted from it is used in medicines prescribed largely for children's ailments, and also for its digestive and relaxant properties.

Common Centaury

This slender plant, formerly known as *Erythraea centaurium*, is the commonest member of its family to be found in the British Isles. It is native to central Europe and is widely distributed throughout Europe and western Asia on dry calcareous soils. It is mainly found on upland

Centaurium erythraea Rafn.
Family GENTIANACEAE

pastures and is a conspicuous plant in late summer amongst the short turf, with its pale leaves and bright pink flowers. It can be either annual or biennial in duration and varies in height from 3–30 cm (1–12 in); the taller plants will be found on the fringe of woodlands or in the shelter of rocky outcrops in hilly or mountainous districts. It has a basal rosette of smooth, strongly veined ovate leaves 2–5 cm ($\frac{4}{5}$–2 in) long and 1–2 cm ($\frac{3}{10}$–$\frac{4}{5}$ in) wide. The stiffly upright stems branch near the top into numerous clusters of flowers.

Uses Centaury has been used since ancient times as a healing herb, both internally for intestinal and stomach complaints and externally for ulcers and skin troubles and for wounds. The legendary centaur of Greek mythology is said to have cured wounds inflicted by poisoned arrows by the use of the juice of this plant. During World War I it was gathered extensively in Great Britain for its healing properties, and it is still collected in continental Europe where it grows in abundance in the upland meadows. The shoots are gathered just as the buds are opening, and the drug obtained from them is used mainly in preparations to stimulate appetite and aid digestion, and as a tonic beneficial to the liver and kidneys. Centaury, once known as 'earth gall', is considered to be the most bitter plant in the Gentianaceae.

Other members of the same family have been used in the past for their healing properties. Richard Le Strange in his *History of Herbal Plants* mentions more than ten species of gentian which have been used in medicine. The most important of these today is the yellow gentian, *Gentiana lutea*. This is a tall plant commonly seen in moist alpine meadows on calcareous soils in Europe. It grows 1·25 m (4 ft) tall and its upright stems carry many pairs of large boat-shaped bracts with dense whorls of short-stalked yellow flowers. The plant is cultivated commercially in Europe and North America for its thick tap root, which may be 60 cm (2 ft) long. This is the gentian root of pharmacy, and after it has been dried and pulverized the drugs are extracted and used in medicinal preparations in tonics and mixtures for various digestive complaints. Gentian violet is a well known preparation in veterinary practice used for cleansing wounds.

The fermented root provides the bitters used in certain alcoholic drinks, particularly in the Swiss liqueur enzian.

Roman Chamomile
True Chamomile

Chamaemelum nobile L.
Family COMPOSITAE

Roman chamomile is a creeping perennial native to southern Europe and nowadays will be found in most regions on dry thin soil in full sun. Under these conditions it is prostrate, a mass of shoots densely covered with finely divided leaves giving the whole plant a moss-like appearance. The lax flower stems are 15 cm (6 in) long. The single flowers are white with conspicuous yellow centres and the double flowers are cream and so full of petals that they resemble small cushions. Two widely differing plants are known by the common name of chamomile; *Matricaria recutita* is the second of them. Several names are used colloquially for this latter plant, eg, sweet false chamomile, German chamomile and true chamomile; it is also known as scented mayweed. Oil is expressed from the dried flowers of both plants, but most herbalists consider that *Chamaemelum* oil is finer. Roman chamomile is thought to be the chamomile referred to by Falstaff in Shakespeare's Henry IV, Part 1, 'the camomile, the more it is trodden on, the faster it grows'. The truth of this dictum is certainly supported by experience of growing the plant.

49

Matricaria recutita L.
Family COMPOSITAE

Cultivation   A well drained site in full sunshine will encourage the dense carpet of shoots; in shade or in heavy, moist land the growth is taller and looser and readily becomes invaded by weeds. All stems in contact with the soil make roots, and propagation can be carried out at any time of the year by pulling the plant to pieces and dibbing them in the ground. The only protection necessary for these cuttings is light shade during periods of bright sunshine. Notes on herb lawns made with chamomile will be found on page 24.

Matricaria recutita is rarely grown in gardens, although it is cultivated in central Europe as a commercial crop. It is very similar to the mayweeds found as common weeds of farm land in the British Isles. All are glabrous plants with finely divided pinnate leaves and white daisy flowers. The true chamomile, while similar, is distinguished from them by its taller growth, 60 cm (2 ft); also the receptacles of its flowers are domed and hollow. The name comes from the Greek 'earth apple', because of the small round heads which are said to smell like apples.

Uses A volatile oil is obtained from both plants, that from *Chamaemelum* being considered the more valuable. It is expressed from the dried young flower heads and prescribed for many ailments such as digestive disorders, muscular spasms and fevers. Herbal tea made from chamomile is recommended as a tonic, a sedative and a cure for colds. Compresses are made from the flowers to ease the pain of burns and inflammation, and the flowers mixed with bruised poppy heads and made into a poultice are said to relieve neuralgia and toothache. Sufferers from insomnia use pillows filled with the dried flowers. A rinse of chamomile is used to lighten fair hair.

Garden Chervil

Anthriscus cerefolium L.
Family UMBELLIFERAE

This very slender annual is a native of southeastern Europe and is found in moist cool valleys. It forms a tiny tap root and the height of the main stem may be only 20 cm (8 in) long in a sunny place but 45 cm (1½ ft) in shade. The stem is ribbed and hollow, and branches freely.

The whole plant is a light green and the leaves are fragile, lacy and fernlike. The pure white flowers grow in flat umbels and the seeds are not unlike caraway seeds but longer and thinner and are a very dark purplish brown when ripe. The whole plant has a fresh, spicy taste similar to that of aniseed.

Cultivation A light, moist, friable soil is essential for this quick growing annual, which tends to run to seed in hot weather or with any check to growth. Chalky or sandy soils which bake hard in periods of drought, or heavy soils which 'pan' in wet weather, should be improved by adding plenty of humus. To maintain a continuous supply of leafy sprigs seed should be sown at monthly intervals, starting in early spring. Crops for summer use should be sown in shade, and for winter use in an open, sunny position. Seed must be sown where the plants are to grow, and seedlings thinned when about 5 cm (2 in) high. The plant has a very short life; in a sunny place it will flower and seed in a few weeks. The duration of one crop can be prolonged by removing flower heads as soon as they appear. Alternatively, if the plants are cut to ground level when about to flower new leaves will grow from the base. If a moist site can be found in a corner of the garden where the plants will not be disturbed, successive crops will grow from self sown seed.

Chervil is not a satisfactory herb to dry under domestic conditions as the application of heat reduces the fragile leaves to an infinitesimal quantity. Steps should therefore be taken to maintain some plants outside for the winter months. An October sowing can be covered by cloches as soon as the weather becomes severe. Plants sown under the protection of a spreading bush such as a gooseberry may survive if the weather is not too cold.

Culinary Use Chervil has a milder flavour than that of most other herbs and should be used in greater quantity. It will improve the quality of almost any dish and also enhances the flavour of other herbs used with it. Its delicate spicy flavour is very volatile, however, and will be lost through long cooking or wilting. For this reason it is always added to a cooked dish in the last few moments of cooking, or if used as a garnish immediately before taking the dish to the table. It may be chopped and used to season cooked savoury dishes, sauces and soups, added to cream cheeses, egg dishes or French dressing, and sprinkled over green or any other vegetable salads. It makes a good alternative to parsley for decoration.

To avoid bruising the leaves when gathering chervil for culinary use it is advisable to take a container rather than bunch them in the hand.

Chives

Allium schoenoprasum L.
Family AMARYLLIDACEAE

These are found growing wild both in Europe and North America. The small, elongated bulbous plants with fresh green, rushlike, tubular leaves grow in tight clusters. There are many forms, the leaves varying in height from 10–20 cm (4–8 in), and the bulbs from 2–8 mm ($\frac{1}{8}$–$\frac{1}{4}$ in). The flowers range in colour from pale pink to rose purple and are carried on hollow stems in attractive clusters in midsummer. The seed is set freely and the whole plant has a mild onion flavour.

Cultivation   These small members of the onion family grow freely on all light, well drained soils but will rot in winter on poorly drained clays. The tight clusters of tiny bulbs need to be divided and replanted every third or fourth year to maintain robust growth. Only the young leaves are required for use in the kitchen, and a continuous supply must be encouraged by cutting plants almost to ground level in rotation throughout the growing season; therefore several clumps will be needed to supply one household. A winter supply can be maintained by covering plants with cloches in autumn. If left untrimmed Chives produce attractive heads of flowers in summer, but these should be removed before the seed ripens or self-sown seedlings will appear all over the garden.

Culinary Use Chives are best used raw as they tend to lose their flavour when cooked. The fresh young growth is chopped and used for flavouring and garnishing any savoury dish. It can be added to cream cheeses or cheese dips, sandwich fillings, salad dressings and sauces, or sprinkled over salads or cooked vegetables. Chives are often preferred by those who find onions too strongly flavoured or indigestible.

Chinese chives, *A. tuberosum* Rottler, are widely grown in China and Japan and are used in the same way as common chives. They are not bulbous plants but have tough rhizomes on the surface of the soil. From these grow thick, flat green leaves 20 × 1 cm (8 × $\frac{1}{3}$ in), and stems 20 cm (8 in) long bearing loose clusters of starry white flowers in loose umbels. These have an attractive appearance and are useful for small flower decorations. The flavour differs from that of true chives. It is less delicate and more similar to garlic.

Colt's-foot

This hardy and persistent perennial with creeping stoloniferous roots is found on moist soils in most regions of the northern hemisphere. It is a conspicuous plant of the early spring. The unbranched scaly flower stems 6 cm (4 in) high are covered with cotton-like fibres and appear in tufts. They each bear a single head of bright yellow flowers with prominent disc florets and numerous thread-like ray florets. The seeds are cylindrical, each with a pappus, and make conspicuous pure white tufts before they scatter. The leaves do not appear until the flowers have faded in late spring. They are perfectly formed when quite small, growing eventually 15–20 cm (6–8 in) in width, broadly ovate with prominent veins, and have uneven, angular, serrated margins; the undersides are densely felted. For several weeks they are a deep olive green, becoming a much paler green in summer. The shape of the

Tussilago farfara L.
Family COMPOSITAE

leaves during the early weeks gives the plant its common name of colt's-foot. The generic name is derived from the Latin word *tussis*, meaning 'cough', an indication of the use to which the plant is put. Colt's-foot is generally found growing on derelict sites, railway banks and roadsides, where the soil is thoroughly compacted, although the stoloniferous roots appear to be soft and fleshy. It would be most unwise to plant colt's-foot in a garden. An immense quantity of seed is produced annually and in addition small fragments of the root will quickly produce a colony of fresh plants.

Uses The majority of ailments said to be cured by the use of colt's-foot are those affecting the chest. The once popular colt's-foot tea was made from the dried flowers, gathered as soon as they were fully open; it was sweetened with honey and taken hot each day to cure a persistent cough. A syrup given in the past to children with chest complaints was made by boiling the dried flowers in water, straining off the liquid and adding liquorice, lemon and honey. The old remedy colt's-foot rock is still sold in the health food stores. It is made by extracting the mucilage from the plant, adding sugar and boiling the mixture until it reaches

55

setting point. The dried leaves are an important constituent of the herbal tobacco recommended to sufferers from asthma; for this the leaves are gathered during the summer and dried and shredded.

Both leaves and flowers are collected from the wild on a commercial scale for the valuable drugs they contain, and after drying are sold to the drug houses.

Coriander

Coriandrum sativum L.
Family UMBELLIFERAE

The name *Coriandrum* is derived from the Greek word meaning 'bug' and the unripe seed has an unpleasant odour, although when fully ripened it has a very pleasant flavour and is highly valued for culinary use. It is indigenous to the Mediterranean but widely cultivated throughout the world, and may be found as a 'garden escape' in most temperate regions. It is a slender, erect, glabrous annual with solid branching stems growing to 50–60 cm (20–24 in). The lower leaves are deeply cut, with ovate segments, and the upper leaves bi-pinnate with segments which are almost thread-like, giving the plant a sturdy and wiry appearance. The umbels of flowers are compound, and the

56

outer flowers, as in so many species in this family, have enlarged petals; they are mainly white but often touched with mauve or red. The fruits are remarkably rounded and ribbed and do not develop their rich, spicy aroma until completely ripe.

Cultivation   As it is essential to obtain fully ripened seed, growing conditions to promote rapid growth must be provided, ie, well drained soil and a sunny position. It is usual to sow the seeds where they are to grow, in late spring when the soil has warmed up, thinning to 10–15 cm (4–6 in) apart as soon as the seedlings are large enough to handle. As with related species of this family, if only a few plants are wanted a pinch of seed could be sown in a few pots, thinning to one seedling per pot and planting them out in late May without breaking the ball of roots. Flowering takes place in July and August, and when fully ripened the seed is harvested as for dill (page 63). It should be stored in an airtight container, where the flavour will improve still further with keeping.

Culinary Use   Before use coriander seed should be crushed or pounded to release the aroma. It is used in the making of curry powder and mixed spice, and is an essential ingredient when these are made in the home. It can be added to bread and spiced cakes and also to soups and casseroles. Seasoned flour can be made for coating veal cutlets and for making apple crumble, and whole seeds can be cooked with stewed fruit. The young roots can be eaten as a vegetable and chopped leaves added to salads and sandwich fillings give them an interesting and unusual flavour.

Other Uses   Coriander is widely used in the canning industry, for flavouring liqueurs and in the manufacture of perfumes. As a herbal remedy it is used as a constituent of a poultice to relieve arthritic and rheumatic pains, and in medicines to combat indigestion and to stimulate the appetite. Its properties resemble those quoted for many related herbs, the constituents of the essential oils being similar in many members of the Umbelliferae family.

Chrysanthemum balsamita L.
Family COMPOSITAE

This is another plant frequently included in the herb garden more for its historical interest than for its present day value as a herb. It is an attractive plant with its silvery green foliage and sweet minty aroma. It has been known by a variety of Latin and common names, and this has led to some confusion over its true identity. Other Latin names that have been used for it in the past are *Tanacetum balsamita*, *Balsamita vulgaris* and *Balsamita major*, but the name given in the heading above is now considered to be valid. Common names given to the plant besides costmary were alecost, allspice, mint geranium, french sage, bible leaf mace and goose tongue (on account of its leaf shape). The name alecost was most commonly used for it in the Middle Ages, when it was in great demand as a bitter flavouring for ale, before the hop came into use for this purpose. The name costmary may be derived from the Greek word *kostos*, Latin *costum*, meaning 'spice', with 'Mary'

referring to the Virgin Mary. The long slender leaf was often used as a book marker in churches, hence the name bible leaf mace.

This perennial and another member of the Compositae, the camphor plant, *Balsamita vulgaris*, both have similar spreading roots and toothed, oblong silvery leaves, 15 × 6 cm (6 × 2½ in), with petioles 15 cm (6 in) long and erect and somewhat woody silvery flowering stems which branch profusely at the top. Here, however, the similarity ends. Costmary has a warm minty aroma and many terminal clusters of apetalous flowers resembling small yellow buttons. The camphor plant has perfect flowers with brilliant white ray petals, and the whole plant has a strong smell of camphor.

Cultivation   Both plants are useful additions to the herb border because of their attractive silvery leaves and their late flowering. Any moisture-holding soil in a sunny position is suitable for them. They grow rampantly and need to be divided and replanted every four to five years. This can be carried out in spring or autumn.

Culinary Use   The leaves of costmary are most useful in the late autumn when the various mint plants have died down. They persist until the frosts become severe and can be used to replace mint in mint sauce. Only very young leaves should be gathered for kitchen use as the bitter flavour becomes more pronounced in the older leaves. When finely chopped they give an interesting new taste to foods and are recommended for adding to salads and other savoury dishes. It can also be used as in the past to flavour home-made beer; and fresh or dried leaves are recommended for making a refreshing tea (but this, like many other herbal teas, is a taste which has to be acquired).

It is often stated that costmary was used in Elizabethan times as a 'strewing' herb to 'sweeten floors and closets'; but it is much more likely that the plant used for this purpose was the camphor plant. The dried leaves are used nowadays for filling moth bags.

Costmary is grown commercially for its roots, which provide a fragrance used in the perfumery trade.

Primula veris L.
Family PRIMULACEAE

These plants, flowering in late spring and early summer, are native to northern and central Europe. They are hardy herbaceous perennials with stout rhizome-like rootstocks and tight rosettes of soft pubescent leaves. These are ovate to oblong, pale green, and irregularly toothed and wrinkled, with winged petioles. The leaf blade and petiole may be as much as 10–15 cm (4–6 in) long. The sturdy flower scapes vary in length from 10–20 cm (4–8 in) and carry a nodding umbel of fragrant yellow flowers with orange lines at the base of the five lobes. The prominent tubular and pleated calyx is toothed, and may be 1·5 cm ($\frac{3}{5}$ in) in length. These attractive plants which were once found in abundance in meadows are now becoming very rare, owing both to the use of selective weedkillers and to the ploughing up of permanent pastures in British farming practice.

Cultivation Although rarely seen in cultivation, cowslips can be raised from seed, but as this must be sown immediately it is ripe it would be necessary to gather it from the wild. Cowslips grow best on light well drained soil, both in sun or partial shade. Once the seedlings are fully grown, as with polyanthus and primulas frequent division of the clumps will keep the plants growing strongly.

Uses In medieval times both the cowslip and the primrose were used to cure a variety of ailments, eg, cramps, convulsions, giddiness, nerve spasms, paralysis and rheumatism. The various remedies were prepared from roots, leaves and flowers.

Today drugs obtained from roots and flowers of cowslips collected throughout Europe are used mainly for respiratory diseases and as sedatives to relieve nervous conditions. An infusion of cowslip flowers is said to cure insomnia, and the popular country beverage cowslip wine is considered to be a good sedative. Unfortunately, preparations for making this wine are tedious, as only the 'pips' ie, corollas, are used and these must be separated from the calyces.

Where the true oxlip, *P. elatior*, grows abundantly, mainly in the European alps, it also is gathered for medicinal use. This plant, once abundant in the eastern counties, is now rarely seen except in limited areas, particularly on the damp chalky clay soils of Suffolk, Essex, Cambridgeshire and Bedfordshire. It can be distinguished from the cowslip by the slender flower scape, the paler and flatter flowers with no orange markings, and the more downy calyx.

The primrose, *P. vulgaris*, in addition to its medicinal uses already mentioned, was used in ointments for skin wounds and rashes. Like the cowslip it is still used in herbal medicine today. An infusion is made from the dried root, or from the fresh plant at flowering time, and administered as a sedative.

Deadly Nightshade

This perennial plant, native to Europe, North Africa and western Asia, will be found on the fringe of woodlands, downland and waste land where the soil is alkaline. It is a herb with a thick knotty rootstock and makes angular and open annual growth 1–1·5 m (3–5 ft) tall. At each node on the branching stems there are two leaves, one large, ovate and entire, 20 × 10 cm (8 × 4 in), and the other small and ending in a sharp apex 10 × 4 cm (4 × 1½ in); both are stalked and a dull dark green. The campanulate flowers are solitary, short-stalked, and pendent from the axils and forks in the branches. They are a pale purplish

Atropa belladonna L.
Family SOLANACEAE

POISONOUS

brown with five spreading lobes and a small calyx. In late summer the large globular fruits ripen and turn a bright, shining violet-black. They are very attractive in appearance, particularly to children, but they are very poisonous. Indeed, **the whole plant is highly toxic and great care must be taken when handling it.**

Uses The two most important drugs obtained from deadly nightshade are atropine and hyoscyamine. The herb is collected from the wild and also cultivated and the plant material is dried and sent to the drug houses for the extraction of these alkaloids. The root is of the greatest value but the stems and leaves are also harvested. The berries are extremely poisonous and are never used. Atropine and hyoscyamine are prescribed for diseases of the eyes and for various disorders of the nervous system and the involuntary muscles. Owing to its high toxicity the plant is not used in herbal medicine, but it is valuable for external use in liniments for the relief of pain in rheumatism and gout.

Its very poisonous nature is reflected in the generic name *Atropa*, which is derived from the Greek name of one of the three Fates, *Atropos*, who cut short the lives of men. Its specific name, *belladonna*, refers to its use by the ladies of medieval Europe, who found that a lotion made from the plant would dilate the pupils of the eyes and so add to their beauty.

Dill

This slender annual, like so many of the freely seeding members of the Umbelliferae, was originally found around the Mediterranean but is now widespread on cultivated soils. It has slender, markedly striated hollow stems growing to 70 cm (28 in). The fresh green foliage is divided into flat, thread-like filaments, the petioles have wide, clasping bases, and the small deep yellow flowers are in large flat or saucer-shaped umbels, often 12 cm (5 in) in diameter. The oval fruits, 4×7 mm ($\frac{1}{6} \times \frac{1}{4}$ in), are ridged and have conspicuous dark lines of oil glands.

Cultivation Dill must be grown on light, well drained soil, in a place where it will be sheltered from wind. Young leaves, young flower stems and seeds are all used. When growing for seed production sowing should be done early, as soon as the soil is warm and friable, to allow plenty of time for growth and thus ensure that the seeds will ripen before the weather becomes cool. If leaves and flower stems only are wanted sowing need not take place until early summer. The seed must be sown where the plants are to grow. Water freely in dry weather. On late cold soils growth may be too slow to allow time for

Anethum graveolens L.
Family UMBELLIFERAE

the seed to ripen. If only a limited number of plants are required, seed could be sown in a seed pan and protected from the cold, and the individual seedlings transplanted while still very young into small pots. When well rooted these should be planted out without further root disturbance. Fresh young growth can be cut for use as required throughout the summer, and the plants harvested when they develop a reddish-purple flush. Cut the entire plant to ground level and hang up in small bunches in an airy place to ripen, placing a cloth underneath to catch the falling seed. Ripening takes place over a long period.

Dill must not be grown in the vicinity of fennel. The two species cross readily and seed from the resultant hybrid plants is less aromatic. Dill and fennel, although superficially similar in appearance, will not be confused if the details mentioned are noted.

Culinary Use   Dill has a pleasant, mild caraway flavour and is a digestant. The leaves can be cooked with a wide range of meat, fish and savoury dishes, or used freshly chopped with cole slaw or potato and other vegetable salads. The flowering stems are added to pickled gherkins and cucumber; whole or ground seeds are used to flavour fish dishes, cream cheese, herb butter and salad dressings, and are cooked with vegetables, especially white cabbage, and sprinkled on bread and apple pie. Dill vinegar is delicious and can be made by the method given on page 30. It should be ready for use in about two weeks.

The flavour of dill seed is delicate and sweet and may be preferred by those who dislike the strong aniseed flavour of caraway. Caraway seed is heavily ribbed and shaped like a new moon, whereas dill seed is a flat oval.

Other Uses   The herb is widely cultivated commercially for use in the food industry. It was used medicinally in the past for its digestive and sedative properties, eg, in the 'gripe water' once commonly and still occasionally given to babies to bring up wind.

Eyebright

Euphrasia rostkoviana Hayne
Family SCROPHULARIACEAE

This small annual is parasitic on grass roots and will be found throughout the northern hemisphere in most of the upland pastures wherever the soil is alkaline. There are a number of very slight differences between the eyebrights found in the same habitat, and until recently these have all been considered natural varieties of the species originally known as *E. officinalis*, but they are now regarded as different species. The chief feature that distinguishes *E. rostkoviana* from the others is the presence of glandular hairs on the upper leaves and on the calyx, and it is these which contain the constituents that are of medicinal value. A feature that would be more clearly visible to the amateur collector is the presence of small lines of brilliant purple on the gleaming white petals. The euphrasias are all erect, branching annuals varying in height from 3–15 cm (1–6 in). They have opposite, toothed leaves, some with indentations deeper than in others. The many flat-faced flowers are lobed, the lower lobe being the larger, and although the flowers are often less than 8 mm ($\frac{1}{3}$ in), and not more than 1·5 cm

($\frac{2}{3}$ in), the flower colour is so vivid and the plants so numerous that these euphrasias are some of the most conspicuous flowering plants to be seen in the turf of the downland and mountain pastures. As this group of plants is semi-parasitic on grass roots and only grows in short dense turf it cannot easily be cultivated.

The generic name comes from the Greek *euphraino* meaning 'to gladden', from its ancient use as a lotion for the eyes. In medieval times, in addition to its continued use for eye troubles, it was used to make tonic drinks, either herbal tea or wine, and it has also been thought to bring relief to sufferers from hay fever.

Uses Eyebright has some uses in modern medicine. The flowering shoots are gathered in the wild and dried for the drug they contain, which has astringent and anti-inflammatory properties. It is still used to make eye washes, and herbal infusions to be taken for digestive and other internal disorders.

The confusion arising from the use of common names for plants is clearly illustrated here. In England another plant, *Salvia sclarea*, was also formerly known by the common name of eyebright. This is a very different plant, a biennial sage, which grows about 75 cm (2$\frac{1}{2}$ ft) tall and is frequently grown in gardens for its striking and attractive pink and purple bracts. The seeds of this plant become coated with a mucilaginous substance when moistened and were once put into the eyes to remove grit and dust; this is a very ancient remedy. The name *sclarea* comes from the Latin *clarus*, meaning clear. This plant is no longer considered to have any value as a healing herb.

Fennel

A native of the Eastern Mediterranean, this is a robust perennial 1·5 m (5 ft) tall, with a thicket of dark green, solid stems, which are rigid and bamboo-like but much branched near the top. The leaves are a fresh green when young, later becoming dark green, and are much divided into fine thread-like segments. The small yellow flowers are in slightly domed umbels. Garden fennel is a selected form of this Mediterranean plant and must not be confused with the fennel found growing on waste land in southern England, with its coarse, dark green foliage and

Foeniculum vulgare Mill.
Family UMBELLIFERAE

rank smell. Garden fennel has more finely divided leaves, a more vivid green colour, and a sweet aroma reminiscent of aniseed. Unless it is grown on a fertile, moisture-retaining soil, however, its growth will be hard and coarse and the aroma less fragrant. The handsome *F.v. nigra*, which has deep copper bronze foliage, is equally aromatic.

Florence fennel, *F.v. dulce*, grown mainly for the swollen leaf bases used as a vegetable, has more feathery, yellowish-green foliage (also used as a herb) and more spreading umbels of flowers.

Cultivation Fennel grows rapidly and in three or four years becomes somewhat woody. A supply of young plants should be maintained by replacement with self-sown seedlings or by division of old plants. Once fennel is established in the garden many self-sown seedlings will be found. Any not required should be removed immediately as they will become difficult to eradicate later. Florence fennel is cultivated mostly in southern Europe and Israel; it tends to run to seed when attempts are made to grow it in cooler climates. Seed is sown annually in summer in a moist sunny position in rich soil, and if it is sown in June running to seed is less likely to occur. In a dry summer it must be kept well watered.

67

Culinary Use The flavour of fennel is very pronounced and only young leaves are used in cookery. The essential oil is a useful digestant and fennel is used to counteract the richness of oily fish such as herrings or mackerel. A few sprigs can be placed inside the fish or it can be grilled on a bed of the leaves. Alternatively chopped leaves can be added to a sauce or stuffing. Chopped fennel is also sprinkled over pork, liver and kidneys before cooking, added to soups, egg dishes, sandwich fillings and salads and to certain vegetables such as beans or cabbage. Umbels of half ripe seeds can be pickled with gherkins and cucumber instead of the usual dill, and crushed ripe seeds are used to flavour savoury dishes and herb bread and biscuits.

One cultivated form, *F.v. peperatum* 'Carosella', has large succulent flower stems which are cut before seeding and peeled and served as a salad with an oil and vinegar dressing.

Other Uses Fennel has long been valued as a health-giving plant; both the Greeks and the Romans made use of it. To-day the seed is collected and dried for its high content of essential oil. This is added to medicines for flavouring, and is used for its digestive properties and as an intestinal disinfectant. Fennel has long been recommended as a herb for slimming as it is thought to reduce the desire for food, but caution is advisable as over use can produce unpleasant side effects.

Oil of fennel is used in the food industry and in the manufacture of toothpastes etc.

Foxglove

Several species of this familiar plant occur in Europe and western Asia, but the common foxglove, *D. purpurea*, is found in the wild mainly in central and western Europe. It is a native plant of acid soils and commonly grows in open woodlands, but providing there is sufficient moisture and shade it will also be found on alkaline soils. It is biennial, and in the first year from seed sowing forms a large rosette of coarsely veined, downy, ovate-lanceolate leaves; this rosette may be 40 cm (16 in) across if growing where there is little competition. In the second year the flowering stems may be 1·25 cm (4–5 ft) tall, with a few scattered small leaves on the lower section and a terminal one-sided raceme of flowers about 30 cm (1 ft) long. The pinkish purple flowers

Digitalis purpurea Ehrh.
Family SCROPHULARIACEAE

POISONOUS

with five lobes are normally 4 cm (1½ in) long and are heavily spotted with deep purple on the inside. They appear from midsummer onwards.

Cultivation It is usual to sow the abundantly produced seed in a seed bed and in early autumn transplant the seedlings to the flowering site; this should be moist and in the shade. The leafy rosettes will grow during the winter and come into flower the following summer. After the first flowering the plant generally dies. Foxgloves are very suitable for a shady corner on the outskirts of the garden, where they can be left to regenerate without disturbance. If used in borders new seedlings will have to be produced and planted out each year.

Use The foxglove was once valued medicinally for its supposed cleansing properties, the juice being used in an ointment for swellings and the bruised leaves applied to grazes and sores. In the sixteenth century, before its very poisonous nature was realized, it was prescribed for various internal complaints, probably with fatal results. In the early nineteenth century it was discovered that cardiac disease could be alleviated by the use of the drug digitalin extracted from the dried and powdered leaves of *D. purpurea*, but the effect of the drug is cumulative and it caused many deaths. Digitalin is still used in modern medicine, but the drug is now obtained mainly from *D. lanata*, a species native to continental Europe, which is less cumulative and is preferred in many cases. *D. lanata* has for some time been appreciated as a flower garden plant. It has larger cream coloured flowers with chocolate brown markings inside the corolla.

Both species are cultivated commercially for the drug houses. **The drugs obtained from both are highly dangerous and are used only under strict medical supervision.**

Garlic

This bulbous perennial has been cultivated from the Mediterranean to central Asia for so long that it is difficult to state its origin. The bulb is enclosed in a white or pinkish transparent skin and when ripened splits into a number of small sections known as 'cloves'. It has a very pervasive aroma. The early spring growth appears as a spike and is composed of enfolded leaves with tubular leaf bases. This growth, with the long strap-like leaves 2·5 cm (1 in) wide with prominent longitudinal veining can eventually be 50 cm (20 in) tall. As the bulbs ripen they appear to be entire, resembling onions, but on drying the outer skins shrivel and split, revealing the individual cloves which are the new crop for culinary use.

Cultivation　The single cloves only are needed for planting, as well as for use in the kitchen, and these are obtained by removing the skins of the main bulb and separating the single segments. These often vary greatly in size and the larger should be selected. A fertile soil is necessary for good growth, but not one that has recently been manured. Late autumn planting in the open is possible in southern England, but it is wiser to delay this until the early spring in regions where the winters are harsh, eg, in northern England. Plant the cloves in a trench or separately with a trowel; they should be placed 5 cm (2 in) deep and 20 cm (8 in) apart. No attention will be required apart from weeding. The bulbs should be harvested in late summer when the leaves are just beginning to turn yellow. Lift with a fork, tie in small bunches, and hang up in a dry, airy place to finish ripening. The bulbs may appear

Allium sativum L.
Family AMARYLLIDACEAE

to be entire at first but will divide into cloves as they dry. If left in the garden until the foliage has become completely yellow they fall apart and the cloves scatter. For storage the bulbs can be made into ropes, as is done with onions, or put into small nets, and stored in a completely dry and frost-proof place.

Culinary Use   The common prejudice some people have against garlic is probably due to over use, but when added sparingly it is a valuable seasoning and can be used in a great variety of savoury dishes. Like onions it contains sulphur and the vitamins A, B and C. According to taste one or two whole cloves or small slivers can be inserted into meat for roasting or grilling or pounded and added to sauces, casseroles etc. A special garlic press can be obtained to extract juice or pulp. A touch of garlic can be added to salad dressings by using garlic vinegar (see page 30) or by putting a few pieces into the prepared dressing. If only a very mild flavour is required, a cut clove should be rubbed round the inside of the casserole or salad bowl.

Other Uses   Garlic is a bactericide and a vermicide. Among its many uses in medicine are the relief of flatulence, the reduction of high blood pressure, and the treatment of bronchial and catarrhal complaints.

Scented Geraniums

Pelargonium species
Family GERANIACEAE

P. tomentosum

P. crispum

P. odoratissimum

Geraniums come mainly from South Africa and botanically speaking are pelargoniums. There are very many species and a few of them have fragrant foliage. These belong to a group known as the rose geraniums, so called because they are used in the perfumery industry. The fragrant essential oils extracted from the leaves are valuable substitutes for the far more costly rose scents. Scented leaved geraniums are widely grown in various areas in northern and southern Africa and on Reunion Island on a commercial basis to supply the industry. These species vary considerably in form and habit and in leaf shape and texture. Some of the plants are markedly upright and some bushy, and others have very lax and sprawling stems. On the whole, members of this group of pelargoniums have small pale-coloured flowers. A few of the leaves of these are illustrated and can be used for flavouring food, eg:

- *P. crispum*, with slender upright stems 30–60 cm (12–24 in) tall, and with lemon scented leaves up to 3 cm ($1\frac{1}{4}$ in) in diameter; there is also a popular variegated form. *P. limonium* is similar but with larger leaves. Both species have strongly indented wavy margins.
- *P. odoratissimum,* with slender branches coming from a woody base, and thin crenate leaves 4 cm ($1\frac{1}{2}$ in) in diameter, which are described as both apple and nutmeg scented.

P. tomentosum, with long, lax, fleshy branches and thick, velvety-textured, deeply lobed, palmate leaves 7 cm (2¾ in) in diameter, strongly peppermint scented. Its prostrate habit makes it more suitable for growing in the garden in summer than as a pot plant; one single plant can make a dense carpet 80 cm (3 ft) wide.

Some other useful fragrant species are *P. capitatum* and *P. graveolens*, both rose scented, *and P. fragrans*, nutmeg scented.

Cultivation   No pelargonium is reliably hardy in the British Isles and these scented plants are grown in the same way as the popular bedding geraniums. In late summer cuttings are taken from that season's flowering growth, inserted in sandy compost, and wintered in a frost-free house, often on window-sills in living rooms. Alternatively, old plants can be lifted and potted, housed for the winter, and replanted in the garden in summer.

Culinary Use   The leaves have a wide range of scent and flavour, and they can be used to add interest to a variety of sweet dishes. One or two leaves may be added to a milk pudding before cooking and to stewed apples and pears or to late rhubarb when its flavour is lessening. Baked apples can be stuffed by placing a rolled-up leaf filled with sultanas and brown sugar in the centre after removing the core. Jams and jellies are flavoured by adding a few leaves to the preserving pan a few minutes before setting point is reached; the leaves should be removed before the mixture is turned out. When making sponges and cakes some enthusiasts place a leaf on the bottom of the tin before filling. Both fresh and dried leaves can be used.

The fragrance of pot-pourri is greatly enhanced by the addition of dried leaves of these scented geraniums.

White Horehound

This plant is found throughout the northern hemisphere as a roadside weed, although it is very localized in Great Britain. It is an herbaceous perennial, with a stout main stem about 45 cm (1½ ft) high; this is erect and square, with spreading branches. These and the dentate, ovate and much wrinkled leaves, 2–5 cm (1–2 in) long and in pairs, are covered with a white cottony wool. The whitish flowers grow in dense clusters in the axils of the leaves. Although not very spectacular, this plant,

Marrubium vulgare L.
Family LABIATAE

with its pale green spikes of pearly white flowers and its long flowering season, helps to furnish the herb border throughout the summer. It flourishes in dry sandy places and gives little trouble in cultivation, but on heavy clay soils the addition of decayed compost is advisable. It is propagated by root division in spring.

Herbal Use   In earlier centuries the plant was thought to be a cure for many widely differing complaints, but the most general use was for coughs and the common cold, chest complaints and whooping cough. It contains a high proportion of mucilage and is cultivated on a small scale and used in the treatment of bronchial and digestive disorders. A well known herbal remedy in bronchial and asthmatic complaints is made by boiling juice extracted from the leaves with an equal amount of sugar until setting point is reached. On cooling this candy is cut into squares, and is very popular for children's ailments. Herbal tea made from *Marrubium* taken daily is said to cause loss of weight.

In the eighteenth century white horehound was used to make a beer. Black horehound, *Ballota nigra*, also a member of the family Labiatae, is a plant with straggling stems and purplish flowers and an objectionable

74

odour, and is unlikely to be mistaken for the white horehound. Black horehound was once believed to be an antidote for the convulsive spasms at the onset of rabies.

Horse-radish

This is a coarse growing perennial with a stout, tapering tap root 60 cm (2 ft) long and 5 cm (2 in) in diameter at the crown. The basal leaves arising from the crown have long petioles, to 15 cm (6 in), and the leaf blades are 45 cm (1½ ft) long and 13 cm (5 in) wide. They are evenly dentated and have markedly wavy margins. The erect flowering stems 75–90 cm (2½–3 ft) tall have almost stemless leaves which are often cut completely to the main vein. The small white flowers in numerous racemes form a spreading terminal panicle.

Horse-radish is a native of southeastern Europe and has become widespread as a garden escape in northern and western Europe.

Armoracia rusticana Gaertn., Mey., Scherb.
Family CRUCIFERAE

Cultivation   Thick fleshy roots are needed for culinary use and roots of satisfactory quality will only be produced on moist fertile soil which has been cultivated deeply. The crop is raised from root cuttings generally known as 'thongs'. These are obtained from the thicker of the side roots 1·5–2 cm ($\frac{1}{2}$–$\frac{3}{4}$ in) in diameter, trimmed from a previous crop when it has been lifted for use. They are cut into lengths 15 cm (6 in) long and prepared with a straight cut at the top and a slanting cut at the lower end. These thongs are stored in bundles in sand during the winter. In early spring they should be planted 30 cm (12 in) apart, placed upright in the soil with the straight cut uppermost, 5 cm (2 in) below the surface. (See also page 20 and fig 9.) Roots will be ready for harvesting in the second autumn after planting. Great care must be taken when harvesting to clear the beds completely of all roots, however small; otherwise the ground will be infested with unwanted plants. The large main roots should be trimmed and stored in clamps for use in the kitchen, and the thongs cut for the next season's planting.

Culinary Use   Horse-radish contains mustard oil and vitamin C; it stimulates the appetite and aids digestion. It is served freshly grated or in a sauce with roast and boiled beef, sausages etc, and with freshwater fish. Horse-radish sauce is made from finely grated roots mixed with cream, salt, pepper and mustard, lemon juice, sugar and vinegar for serving cold; a sauce to be served hot can be made by mixing the same ingredients with béchamel sauce.

Other Uses   The plant is used in medicine for bronchial complaints, and as a tonic and a digestant. It is also used in external applications for rheumatism, but can have an irritant effect on some skins.

Hyssop

This small and occasionally almost prostrate subshrub rarely grows more than 20 cm (8 in) tall, and has a profusion of short branches. Its habit differs greatly according to the type of soil on which it is growing; on well drained soil it grows as a small upright shrub and will be evergreen in most winters, but on heavy compact soil it makes a low, dense cushion of growth spreading over the soil and is deciduous.

Hyssopus officinalis L.
Family LABIATAE

The small grooved flowering stems are covered with narrow, oblong, dark green leaves. They terminate in closely packed whorls of small purplish-blue flowers all facing to one side, thus making a brush-like spike. The plant continues to flower into late autumn. There are also white and pink forms, but neither is so free growing nor so attractive as the type plant.

Cultivation Hyssop is found growing on the exposed southern slopes of the mountainous regions of the Mediterranean coast, and this habitat gives an indication of its cultural requirements. In gardens with sloping ground a suitable place could be made for it in a sheltered sunny position by the use of a few large bricks or stones. Alternatively, the sides of a concrete or gravel path would provide satisfactory conditions. The hyssop could be planted at the edge and allowed to sprawl over the surface to break the hard line. The plant has a long flowering period which continues late into the autumn, and as it is rather tender it should not be cut back until the following year when new growth is evident. Then trim with shears to remove all the previous year's dead flowering stems, cutting lightly into growing wood. As old plants are generally less winter hardy than young ones they should be replaced as soon as they become woody. Often small rooted shoots can be separated from the parent plant and kept in a

77

shady place until well established; the separation should be carried out in spring with the aid of a hand fork. An alternative method is to make cuttings of well ripened shoots of the current year's growth. These can be stripped from the bush, inserted in a cold frame and treated as half ripe cuttings. If well rooted they can be planted in the open the following spring.

Culinary Use   Hyssop is not a popular herb in the kitchen but some are very enthusiastic about using it. Sheila Howarth, in her recent book *Herbs with Everything* (1977), suggests many uses for the chopped young leaves and flowers, eg, in soups, stews, stuffing and white sauces, cottage cheese, meat, fish and poultry, salads and vegetables, fruit pies and cocktails. Her book gives many appetising recipes for this strong, peppery herb, but warns against its over use.

Other Uses   Hyssop has long been used as a remedy for indigestion and its spicy oil is used in medicines for stimulating the appetite. Herbal tea made from the dried flowers is used for chest complaints, and a gargle from flowers and leaves to relieve sore throats and colds. In former times the clipped summer growth of the herb was used with other 'strewing' plants for covering floors before the days of carpets; the strong smelling volatile oil released was thought to be a useful deterrent of fleas and lice. The oil distilled from the flowering tips is used at the present time in the manufacture of liqueurs and in perfumery.

Insect Powder Plant

This herbaceous perennial is native to parts of Yugoslavia, particularly the region once known as Dalmatia, hence the common name Dalmatian pyrethrum. As with all the group of plants commonly known as pyrethrums, the perennial cushion of basal growth is about 20 cm (8 in) high and is made up of hundreds of densely packed slender plantlets. In this particular species the finely cut silvery grey leaves are 15–20 cm (6–8 in) long, petiolate and oblong in outline. The solitary white flowers are approximately 2·5 cm (1 in) in diameter and are carried on wiry, grey stems, 30–45 cm (12–18 in) long.

Chrysanthemum cinerariifolium Trév.
(syn. *Pyrethrum cinerariifolium*)

Family Compositae

Cultivation   This plant is hardy in the south of England and grows best on calcareous soils and sandy, well drained sites. It is perfectly hardy on lime-free clays but becomes somewhat unkempt in appearance. The silvery mounds persist through most winters. From midsummer for several weeks the pure white flowers are produced in abundance, making the plant a highly decorative addition to the herb border. The densely packed plants need to be divided frequently if free flowering is to be maintained. This should be done in spring during damp weather, as soon as active growth becomes apparent. If the plants are disturbed in the autumn and the following winter is very wet and cold they may not survive. The flowers last well in water and are very useful for small flower arrangements.

Uses   The use of several species of pyrethrum as insecticides originated in Persia (Iran), and in the nineteenth century *C. cinerariifolium* was selected as the most effective for this purpose. The plant is now grown commercially in a number of countries in warm regions, the most important of these being Japan and Yugoslavia. For commercial crops the plants are raised from seed and the flowers are gathered in the third, fourth and fifth years; after this period the yield declines and the old plants are replaced by seedlings. The flowers are picked without stems when they are three-quarters open, and are then dried and crumbled. Dusts and also sprays containing the essential oil are used as insecticides, especially where it is necessary to use non-poisonous deterrents on food crops. These insecticides were widely used in World War II against malaria-carrying mosquitoes, and pyrethrum aerosols are used in passenger aircraft.

Pyrethrum will kill all cold-blooded creatures and must not be used near pools containing fish. Prolonged handling of pyrethrum dust can cause dermatitis and asthma, and if it is being used continuously the wearing of gloves and respirators is recommended.

Juniper

Juniper is one of the few conifers native to the British Isles and is widespread over the whole of the northern hemisphere. It is most usually found as a much branched and twiggy, spreading, evergreen bush or erect shrub, 1·5–2 m (5–6 ft) tall, but may grow into a tree up to 8 m (24 ft) high. The reddish wood is densely clothed with stiff, awl-shaped leaves which terminate in a sharp point; these are concave on the upper surface with a glaucous band up the centre and the under surface is keeled and green. The fruits are globose, 6 mm ($\frac{1}{4}$ in) in diameter, black and covered with a grey-blue bloom, and contain 2–3 seeds embedded in the mealy, resinous pulp. These usually take three years to ripen.

Cultivation Juniper grows best on lime soils but will tolerate others. It is dioecious, ie, the male and female flowers are on separate plants, the female flowers forming minute catkins and the male being shield-like scales bearing the anthers. As it is a spreading plant and two are required for the production of fruit juniper is only suitable for the larger gardens. The seed has a dormancy period of at least one year, but germination can be hastened by putting it in boiling water for a few seconds to soften the seed coat.

Only the berries of the true species of juniper yield the high quality volatile oil. The various dwarf forms and hybrids often fail to flower

Juniperus communis L.
Family CUPRESSACEAE

♂ ♀

or the oil they produce, if any, is poor in quality. The common juniper is seldom planted in a garden and the berries are normally purchased from a herb shop, or may be gathered in the wild in early autumn by shaking the branches over a canvas sheet. The harvested berries are spread out thinly and left in a shady, airy place until they have shrivelled slightly. They are then stored in an airtight container, but are best used within a year of harvesting as they become dry and lose their flavour if kept too long.

Culinary Use   Juniper berries are used either fresh or dried to flavour poultry and game and all meats, especially pork and ham, and are added to casseroles, patés, sauces, sauerkraut and pickles. About six berries would be required for a dish for four persons. It is usual to crush them slightly before use. Juniper wood is used in the curing of smoked meats. In the Netherlands and France the essential oil is used to give gin its characteristic flavour. This accounts for its name, which is derived from the Old French *genevre* (O.E.D). English gin is usually flavoured with a substitute.

Other Uses Oil of juniper extracted from the berries is used in the treatment of rheumatism and as a digestant. It is included in ointments for the relief of rheumatic pain and in bath oils. A well known remedy for rheumatism is 1–2 drops of juniper oil taken daily on a lump of sugar, and a widely recommended country cure for the same complaint consists of soaking young tips of juniper shoots in cold water for several hours, then boiling them for three hours and adding the strained solution to bath water. It should be noted that sufferers from kidney complaints are warned never to take juniper oil in any form, neither should it be taken during pregnancy.

Lavender

Like so many of our well known herb plants, the common lavender is native to the stony, well drained soils of the Mediterranean region. It grows approximately 60 cm (24 in) tall, and the narrowly oblong-linear leaves, 3–5 cm (2 in), with rolled margins, are grey above and distinctly white below. The ribbed annual stems carrying the flower spikes are about 30 cm (12 in) long with opposite oblong leaves; these leaves are usually twice as long as those on the main part of the shrubby plant. The 1 cm ($\frac{2}{5}$ in) long greyish blue flowers are in whorls forming an interrupted spike usually 8 cm (3 in) long. The lavenders most commonly grown in gardens are forms of *L. angustifolia*, varying from round, densely packed shrubs only 30 cm (1 ft) high to vigorous bushes 75 cm ($2\frac{1}{2}$ ft) high. Flower colour can vary from grey-blue to deep purple, pink or white. *L. latifolia*, a similar plant with wider leaves 1 cm ($\frac{2}{5}$ in) and densely tomentose all over, is less hardy in England; it was once known as *L. spica*. *L. stoechas*, sometimes known as French lavender or 'Stic-a-dore', is a smaller and sparser growing shrub with greenish grey leaves speckled with light brown, 2 cm × 3 mm ($\frac{3}{4}$ × $\frac{1}{8}$ in). The short flower spikes have four distinct rows of deep purple flowers with a tuft of pinkish purple bracts at the tip. It is found growing freely on the steep mountainsides in the south of France.

Cultivation *L. angustifolia* grows best and produces the finest fragrance when grown on well drained but moisture-retaining soils in a sunny place. There are several varieties of this common lavender: 'Grappenhall', a robust plant with deep lavender blue flowers; 'Old English', highly scented; and 'Dutch Lavender' with remarkably grey

Lavandula angustifolia Mill.
(*Lavandula officinalis* L.)

Family LABIATAE

leaves. When compact, low growing bushes are required 'Hidcote', with violet coloured flowers, or 'Munstead', with lavender blue flowers could be chosen, both with narrow leaves; neither of these varieties, however, is so fragrant as the first-mentioned varieties. The species *L. latifolia* has a sweet and enjoyable scent although the oil, known commercially as 'spike lavender' oil, is inferior to that of *L. angustifolia*. *L. stoechas* is hardy in cool climates only if grown on very poor, stony soil in a sheltered position. Self sown seedlings are frequently to be found in the vicinity of the parent plant. It is grown for its attractive appearance rather than for its scent.

To keep lavender bushes compact and shapely they must be clipped over with shears to the base of the flowering stems as soon as the flowers have been gathered or have faded. If this is not done in late autumn it can be done just as the new growth starts in spring. Lavender is a short lived plant and needs to be replaced after 5–7 years. It is readily propagated by tearing small slips of ripened shoots from a healthy plant and inserting these in sandy soil in the open ground in late summer. One year later they can be planted finally.

Use Lavender is cultivated on a field scale for the highly aromatic essential oil which is distilled from the flowers; in Europe the most important centre for this is in the south of France. In the home the

83

dried flowers are used to fill sachets for scenting drawers and cupboards, and their long lasting fragrance makes them indispensable for pot pourri. To obtain the maximum fragrance flower spikes for drying must be gathered just before the first flowers are fully opened. They should be cut with their long stems, and can be dried by spreading them in thin layers on a cloth in a warm, shaded room, or by hanging them in small bunches from the rafters in an attic. After three or four weeks the flowers will rub easily from the stalks and are then sieved to remove bracts and dust. When handling them in any quantity gloves and a face mask should be worn for this dusty task.

Lemon Balm

Melissa officinalis L.
Family LABIATAE

An herbacaeous perennial with thick, matted, wiry roots. The numerous slightly hairy square stems, 60–80 cm (24–30 in) tall, branch freely, making a dense, lush growth. This growth is crowded with pairs of rounded ovate, light green leaves, 5 × 3 cm (2 × 1¼ in), and deeply veined; this gives them a wrinkled appearance, making the thin leaf look thicker and more substantial than it really is. Insignificant creamy flowers, both male and female, grow in loose bunches in the axils of the upper leaves throughout the summer. The whole plant has a lemony scent when bruised. This plant comes from the moist and fertile lowlands of central and southern Europe and the regions surrounding the Mediterranean.

Cultivation   There is no comparison between lemon balms grown on light soils in the sun and those which are grown on moist soils shaded in the hottest part of the day. The latter have fresh green foliage with a fresh lemony fragrance, whereas the former have yellowish green leaves and a harsh aroma. Young plants are preferable for the same reason, and after three or four years the old and by now large, overcrowded bushes should be replaced. Propagation is by division of the old plants, ie, by splitting off pieces of the outer growth with surface runners attached, or by selecting young seedlings invariably to be found in the vicinity of the parent plants. As a garden feature the fresh green, free growing new plants are so much more attractive in appearance. Lemon balm is very attractive to bees and for this reason is also known as bee balm. The generic name *Melissa* comes from a Greek word associating the plant with bees. In cottage gardens it has been the custom for bee keepers to plant lemon balm in quantity round their beehives.

Culinary Use   This source of lemon flavouring has largely been superseded by the introduction of real lemons, but the herb can be used in the majority of dishes where a lemon flavour is needed, either as fresh or as dried leaves. A greater quantity will be required than is usual with most herbs as the flavour is delicate. Chopped leaves can be used in stuffings for pork, veal or poultry, in soups and stews, marinades and sauces and with egg dishes. Freshly picked young leaves may be added to green salads, fruit salads and wine cups and a few sprigs cooked with stewed apples or rhubarb impart a flavour which is pleasantly lemony without being acid. In the Middle East it is customary to serve a 'tisane' made by infusing a small handful of young shoots in boiling water; this is sweetened to taste and is considered to be a refreshing tonic at the end of a hot day. A few sprigs can be added to a cup of milkless tea in place of the more usual slice of lemon.

Lemon balm can be dried successfully if young leaves are picked at flowering time when they will have the maximum fragrance. They need to be handled with care to avoid bruising, and if dried in the shade will retain their full aroma. They are a useful addition to pot pourri or to a mixture of herbs for sachets or pillows. The essential oil is used commercially as a constituent of various liqueurs.

Aloysia triphylla L'Herit.
Family VERBENACEAE

Although this is a tender plant introduced into Europe from South America in the late eighteenth century, it will survive out of doors in southeastern England in most winters if grown in a sheltered place. In the west country and the Isle of Wight it can be seen growing as a twiggy shrub 1·5–2 m (5–6 ft) high in the open, and in the Channel Islands it grows 3–3·5 m(10–14 ft) high. The young wood is purplish, becoming greener as it grows older; the previous year's wood is straw-coloured with a pronounced silvery sheen, and the much older wood is generally scarious. The lanceolate leaves taper to a fine point and are mostly in threes, although occasionally they come in fours. They are a fresh light green with adpressed bristles along the margins, and are dotted with oil glands on both sides. These glands are so small that they can only be seen with the aid of a lens, but if the leaves are handled their presence is very obvious. The tiny white or lavender coloured flowers have spreading lobes and are scarcely 0·5 cm ($\frac{1}{4}$ in) in diameter. They are in compound axillary and terminal spikes.

Lemon verbena is a native of Chile and Argentina and was introduced into Europe by the Spaniards. At one time it was known as

Lippia odorata and was so named after the French traveller Dr Auguste Lippi.

Cultivation   On thin and exceedingly well drained soils, and if planted where it will receive maximum sunshine, this shrub withstands most cold winters. An ideal site would be at the foot of a wall at the south west corner of a building in very poor soil. In severe winters the top growth will be killed to ground level, but normally new shoots will eventually grow from the crown late in the next year. No tender shrub should ever be cut back late in the summer as this would encourage new growth which will not ripen before the onset of winter. Also the previous season's twiggy growth acts as a protection for the crown of the plant, shielding it from frost damage. Old plants are always more vulnerable in adverse conditions, and it is wise as a precaution to propagate lemon verbena at intervals of 5–6 years. Both soft and hard wood cuttings root easily during the summer. The rooted cuttings should be kept indoors during the first winter and not planted out until the spring.

Culinary Use   The strongly lemon scented leaves can be used as a substitute for lemons when these are scarce or expensive, although they lack the acidity. They can be used to flavour cakes and stewed fruit and in drinks, and in any dish where lemon is used purely as a flavouring. Fresh or dried leaves are used to make a fragrant and refreshing tea, but it is advisable not to use lemon verbena too frequently as it may cause gastric irritation.

Other Uses   It retains its aroma when dried for several years, and is invaluable as a scented leaf for pot-pourri and herb sachets. The essential oil is used in the perfumery industry.

Lovage

A remarkably handsome, strong growing perennial 2 m (6–7 ft) tall when flowering. This is native to southern Europe and Asia, and is widely grown elsewhere for its rich, yeasty flavour. It is a true herbaceous perennial, dying to ground level each autumn; in spring rich copper coloured shoots emerge from the fleshy, spongy rootstock. As the plant grows these shoots become deep green. The leaves, which

87

may be up to 80 cm (30 in) wide on long succulent petioles, resemble those of a large celery. Numerous umbels of greenish yellow flowers are borne on stiffly upright hollow stems 2 m (6 ft) high. The large oblong seeds are conspicuously winged and when ripe are brown and woody. This latter feature distinguishes lovage from a somewhat similar native plant, alexanders or black lovage, *Smyrnium olusatrum*, which has black seeds and in former times was used as a culinary and medicinal herb.

Cultivation   When grown on heavy soils lovage easily attains its full height; on light free-draining soils it may be far shorter unless plenty of humus is added for the retention of moisture. Waterlogging in winter is fatal, causing the fleshy roots to rot. Shelter and sun are essential for successful growth. This tall plant is only suitable for the back of the border and needs plenty of space. For a continuous supply of good growth division will probably be needed every 3 to 4 years. This is carried out in early spring just as new growth is emerging; it is unwise to disturb the roots in the autumn as to do so may also cause rotting during the winter when growth is dormant. Division is carried out with a sharp spade or knife as the prongs of a fork may damage the tough fleshy roots and cause decay. A piece of root with 3–4 buds will form a new plant.

Levistichum officinale Koch
Family Umbelliferae

Culinary Use Lovage has a distinctive rich flavour which adds body to any savoury dish. Leaves, stems, roots and seeds are all used. If a few can be spared, the emerging shoots, when 10–12 cm (4–5 in) long, are delicious eaten like celery or with an oil and vinegar dressing. Young leaves may be added to salads or crushed in the hand and rubbed over the skin of a frozen chicken to improve the flavour, and two or three short lengths of the succulent leaf stalks can be added to casseroles and soups. Any tender roots left over after division can be boiled and served with French dressing, and a pleasant sweetmeat may be made by candying the young stems. The dried seeds store well for winter use and can be put into muslin bags for use in soups or stews and added to herb breads and biscuits. The leaves also dry well and retain a pleasant green colour and a good flavour. Unlike most herbs, Lovage is put into the dish at the commencement of cooking, but as it is strongly flavoured only small amounts are required.

Other Uses In the sixteenth and seventeenth centuries the dried root was powdered and mixed with wine as a cure for flatulence, and the seeds were chewed to aid digestion. Lovage is still used in a variety of herbal cures, eg, as a laxative or for the treatment of internal inflammatory disorders. It is also used externally for poulticing, and when added to a bath is said to improve the circulation and stimulate the action of the kidneys. A pleasant and relaxing broth can be made from any part of the plant.

French or Pot Marjoram

This species is native to Sicily, southeastern Europe and Asia Minor, but although it comes from these warmer climates it is hardy and can be grown as a perennial in temperate regions. A thicket of slender, wiry stems 27 cm (10 in) high arises from a densely matted and wiry rootstock. The ovate leaves, rarely more than 2·5 cm ($\frac{3}{4}$ in) long, are a fresh light green and persist in a leafy mat throughout the winter. The pale flesh-coloured flowers are in dense clusters in ovoid spikelets. French marjoram has a more delicate flavour than common marjoram (oregano – see page 93).

Origanum onites L.
Family LABIATAE

Cultivation   This is a useful little plant as it remains green for most of the year, and although it is not of much value as a culinary herb once the flowering period has finished it furnishes the herb border during the winter months when most plants are underground. French marjoram is exceedingly easy to grow if given the right conditions; it needs more moisture than other species of marjoram normally grown. On thin chalky or sandy soils well decayed humus should be worked into the site when preparing the ground. On naturally moist soils and clays the low growing mats extend rapidly and in a small herb garden this spreading growth will need to be kept in check by frequent division. A stock of plants can be raised from seed by sowing directly where the plants are to grow, but germination is slow and the small plants may easily become smothered by weeds and it may be wiser to sow the seed in a seed box. However, once a stock of plants has been acquired vegetative propagation can be carried out by division. This is usually carried out in the early autumn as the shallow rooted plants may suffer from drought if disturbed in spring.

French marjoram is a reasonably small herb to grow indoors for a winter supply, especially as it develops a stronger aroma in a warm atmosphere.

Culinary Use   Although the flavour of French marjoram is stronger than that of the common marjoram found growing wild in many dry places in England, it is much milder than that of the same common marjoram when grown in the Mediterranean regions and sold by the trade in the dried form under the name of oregano. It is therefore useful when a less pungent marjoram is desired. It can be used fresh in a *bouquet garni* or for adding to salads and vegetables or other savoury dishes, or dried in home-made herb mixtures. The unopened flower heads, which have more aroma than the leaves, can be used during the short season they are available either fresh or for drying for winter use.

Sweet or Knotted Marjoram

Origanum majorana L.
Family LABIATAE

Sweet marjoram with its very upright habit is markedly different from the two other marjorams grown in the herb garden, both of which make a mat of prostrate roots forming a carpet from which the annual shoots arise. It comes from North Africa, the Middle East and some regions of India. In its native habitats it is perennial, with a compact, woody basal growth, and grows 30–60 cm (1–2 ft) tall with much-branched stems; but in all temperate climates it is treated as a half hardy annual and usually grows 45 cm (18 in) tall. The light green stems and foliage are often covered with fine white hairs. The elliptical, prominently veined leaves, generally 3 × 1 cm ($1\frac{1}{4}$ × $\frac{1}{3}$ in), are stalked on the lower but sessile on the upper shoots. The flowers are in tight clusters at the ends of short branches, and while in bud are protected by broad leafy bracts; these enclosed clusters resemble green balls or 'knots'. The individual flowers, which scarcely emerge from the ball of bracts, are small and threadlike; they may be white, pale lilac or pink.

Cultivation Sweet marjoram must be treated as other half hardy annuals. Most commonly the seed is sown in a frost-free place in spring, pricked out and kept in a frame until the weather is sufficiently warm for planting outside. When it is not possible to raise plants with protection, seed can be sown outside once the danger of severe frost has passed. If the land is prepared for seed sowing some time in advance and covered with cloches or a sheet of polythene, this will warm the soil and hasten germination. Thin the seedlings to 25 cm (9 in) apart. Sweet marjoram needs a light friable soil with plenty of humus to promote rapid growth. A winter supply of fresh marjoram can be provided by potting plants in sandy soil in early autumn and keeping them indoors on a sunny window-sill.

Culinary Use Sweet marjoram has a more subtle flavour than either oregano (*O. vulgare*), or French marjoram (*O. onites*) and as it is less pungent can be used more lavishly. It is used with most savoury dishes, either on its own or in herb mixtures. Chopped leaves can be sprinkled over a roasting joint during cooking, or over vegetables such as brussels sprouts, cabbage and carrots just before serving. Lettuce and other vegetable salads are made more interesting with small additions of this herb. It is this marjoram with its less pronounced flavour which is used in the commercial mixed herbs, and it is equally useful for the home produced mixtures.

Other Uses Marjoram is used in medicine mainly to improve digestion, and is prescribed by herbalists for asthma and coughs. An oil extracted from this herb, *oleum majoranae*, is recommended for application to bruises.

Wild Marjoram or Oregano

This is a very extensively distributed species growing wild in a wide range of habitats, Europe, the Middle East, the Himalayas and Iran, and cultivated practically everywhere except in the tropics. It is a very variable species in all characteristics, height, leaf form, flower colour, etc. In the British Isles this is the plant called 'marjoram' and in Italy it is the much used aromatic herb 'origano'. The plants growing in southern Europe have a far stronger essential oil than those growing in cooler climates; the aroma of the latter is scarcely discernible and has little culinary value. Marjoram varies considerably with different habitats, and even in one single habitat there can be several variations. In a short stroll along the chalk cliffs of southeastern England it is possible to find a large number of forms with widely differing flower and leaf colour.

The plant is perennial, with a tangled, rhizomatous, woody rootstock; from this arise wiry leaf stems 20–30 cm (8–12 in) tall. In Great Britain these die almost to the ground each year. The leaves are opposite and decussate, ovate and pointed, 2–4 cm ($\frac{3}{4}$–$1\frac{1}{2}$ in) long with short

Origanum vulgare L.
Family LABIATAE

petioles, and are either hairy or smooth. The flowers are in spreading terminal corymbs and vary in colour from pale pink to deep magenta; they have glandular calyces and conspicuous purple or greenish bracts. They appear from late summer to early autumn. In the Mediterranean regions the plant does not die entirely each year but becomes a twiggy subshrub.

Cultivation   As wild marjoram is found on chalky or gravelly soils on cliffs or roadside banks, in cultivation it needs a well drained site in full sun and shelter from cold winds. As it is included in the herb garden more for its attractive appearance than for its value as a kitchen herb, the more colourful types should be selected whenever possible. The plants can be raised from seed or propagated by division in spring.

Several other species of origanum with a stronger aroma than that of *O. vulgare* are found in the Mediterranean regions and give their distinctive flavour to the local cooking. *O. dictamnus* (dittany of Crete) is one of these. It is a sprawling plant with thin leaves which are much rounded at the base and have prominent veins. The clusters of flowers are in drooping cones with large sheathing bracts, resembling those of the hop plant. The long pink flowers appearing in late summer protrude from the bracts. Dittany of Crete is not reliably hardy in England but will survive most winters if grown in a wall so that no moisture can rest in the crown of the plant, and where it will be well baked by hot sunshine. *O. dubium* is another example. This is a greyish green shrub with a woody base, highly aromatic. It needs to be wintered in a frost free place. It is the origani used in Greece and has an even more powerful aroma than the Italian herb.

Culinary Use   Oregano imported commercially in dried form from southern Europe has a strong and distinctive flavour and is used mostly on its own. It is more suitable than the sweeter and milder French and sweet marjorams for use in Mediterranean style cookery, eg, in meat sauces for pasta or in sausages or vegetable soups. A light sprinkling of it gives a green salad a refreshingly unusual touch.

Other Uses   A mild tonic is prepared from marjoram, and herbalists recommend fresh or dried tips for making a herbal tea to relieve nervous headaches. When fresh leaves are obtainable they can be tied in muslin and added to bath water and are said to ease rheumatic pains.

An attractive reddish or purplish brown dye is obtainable from the flowering tops of *O. vulgare*, and this is used by home dyers to dye sheep's wool.

Marsh-mallow

Althaea officinalis L.
Family MALVACEAE

This salt-tolerant plant is commonly found in the estuaries of tidal rivers and marshy inlets around the coast. It is a native of temperate Europe and Asia and is now widespread in all temperate regions throughout the world. In the countryside it is an arresting plant with its silvery white growth; the whole plant is covered with a soft, dense velvety down. The main stem, as a rule, is erect and branching, growing approximately 1 m (3 ft) tall. The stalked leaves are only rarely lobed and are shallowly toothed, the lower ones cordate at the base and the upper narrower, both coming to a point at the apex. A distinguishing feature of the marsh-mallow is the presence of five or more bracts below the five-lobed flower calyx. The pale pink flowers are in loose clusters in the leaf axils at the base of the stems and in terminal leafless spikes. The roots are fleshy but tough and spreading.

The common mallow, *Malva sylvestris* L., is a closely related plant with only three bracts below the calyx. The magenta pink flowers are in loose axillary clusters but seldom in terminal spikes and have five narrow petals, strongly veined and deeply notched at the apex. When fully open these colourful flowers are star-like in appearance. The leaves are long stalked and rounded in outline, with five or seven lobes and cordate at the base; they have only a few scattered hairs and are green,

not silvery as those of the marsh-mallow. The roots of *M. sylvestris* are very fibrous, not fleshy. It is seldom seen as an upright bushy plant. More generally its growth is spreading and intermingled with the herbage growing on the poor dry soils of stony banks, roadsides and waste land well away from the sea coast.

Culinary Use   Marsh-mallow was once cooked as a vegetable and today the fresh young tips of the shoots are used as an addition to salads. It has given its name to the well known sweetmeat, marsh-mallow, which was once made from its dried and powdered root.

Other Uses   Both the marsh-mallow and the common mallow are a source of mucilage, a viscous gummy substance occurring in many plants, with emollient and healing properties. This is obtained in large amounts from the roots of marsh-mallow, both from wild and specially cultivated plants. The commercially grown plants are harvested in their second year for the extraction of the mucilage. The leaves also are collected; the best time for this is immediately before flowering. The stringy fibrous roots of common mallow are not used, but the leaves and flowers are collected.

In southern Europe a strong growing subspecies of *M. sylvestris* is grown for its leafage. This is *M.s.* ssp *mauritiana*. It makes an upright free branching bush with large, showy deep pink flowers and is often seen as a decorative plant in English gardens.

Both mallows yield other useful constituents in addition to mucilage. The drugs are prescribed for various complaints such as bronchitis and asthma, and an ointment is made for minor wounds and chilblains. A syrup for sore throats popular with children is made by boiling the roots of the marsh-mallow in water and adding honey to the strained liquid.

Meadow Saffron (Autumn Crocus)

This species of *Colchicum* is a native of Europe and western Asia and will be found growing on deep pasture land. One of its common names, autumn crocus, leads it to be confused with the true crocus, but it is a member of the Liliaceae family while the true crocus belongs to the Iridaceae. Colchicums have large bulbs resembling those of tulips in size and shape but less compact; they are loose and untidy in appearance. The outer scale is brown, thick and leathery, and is liable to separate from the fleshy scales beneath. The pinkish-purple flowers appearing in the autumn rise 8–10 cm (3–4 in) above the ground on a long corolla tube which expands into six segments 5–8 cm (2–3 in) in length. There are six stamens and three long threadlike styles. The ovary is superior and within the base of the corolla tube which has remained below ground; as the seeds ripen the very short flower stem lengthens, bringing the seed capsule up to the surface of the soil.

The chief characteristics of the true crocus are very different. The root is a true corm, small and generally flattened, and the outer tunic is fibrous and often netted. The leaves, grasslike in appearance, generally appear with the flowers and these have only three stamens and one style with three stigmatic lobes which are generally dilated, cut, and fringed at the top. The ovary is inferior, ie, below the base of the corolla tube.

Some confusion may arise as there are a number of the true crocus species which also flower in the autumn, but these closely resemble the familiar spring flowering crocus.

Colchicum autumnale L.
Family LILIACEAE

POISONOUS

Cultivation   A deep, moist and fertile soil is necessary for colchicums. As plants raised from seed may take three or four years to flower it is usual to purchase bulbs. These increase freely and should be lifted and divided every four or five years, this task being done about June after the leaves have died down.

Use   The cures that can be achieved by the use of the drug obtained from *C. autumnale* have been known for many centuries, but it is very poisonous and the dangers of using it are so great that it was rarely prescribed. About two hundred years ago German scientists working on the problem solved the difficulties of administering it safely, and colchicum is now grown commercially for the drug houses. The most important constituent extracted from the bulbs and leaves is colchicine. The drug is used to relieve the inflammation and pain of acute forms of rheumatism and gout. It is administered in the form of pills, but only under strict medical supervision.

Colchicine is also used in plant breeding in the development of giant strains, owing to its property of inhibiting cell division.

A number of species of the genus *Colchicum* are grown as garden plants, flowering during the autumn and winter, or very early in the spring.

Garden Mint or Spearmint

The mints are widely distributed throughout Europe, and it is commonly thought that the garden mint, *Mentha* x *spicata*, was introduced into northern and western Europe by the Romans. It is also commonly called spearmint, lamb mint or pea mint. There is a wide variation in the garden mints and it is difficult to describe them precisely. Some have green stems and smooth, fresh green leaves, some purple stems and leaves flushed with bronze-purple, and some are slightly hairy. The annual shoots grow 15–30 cm (6–12 in) tall, and the opposite, lanceolate, toothed leaves may be blunt-ended or sharp-pointed, thick or thin in texture, and hairy or smooth. In late summer these shoots bear lilac-coloured flowers in cylindrical spikes. The aroma also varies considerably and it is advisable when stocking up the garden to select the finest form that is obtainable.

Cultivation   A position in half shade is necessary. The bed should be prepared with well decayed compost, and the runners laid in shallow drills 5 cm (2 in) apart. Planting can be done either in spring or autumn. When the top growth dies down in autumn it should be removed and a further mulch of compost applied. To maintain the mint bed in full production and the plants free from disease they need to be re-planted every 3–4 years. Rust, the most common disease of mint, is more likely to attack old and crowded plants. This is clearly recognizable from the appearance of orange-coloured pustules on the undersides of the leaves; in a bad attack the stems and overground runners are severely distorted. If the infected shoots are not removed the spores fall to the ground and infect all the runners. A light attack of this disease of mint can be controlled by packing the dying shoots with dry straw and burning it, following with the autumn mulch. When it becomes necessary to replant the bed it is best to select a new site and replant only vigorous disease-free runners.

All mints are very invasive and it is a good plan to restrict root growth by surrounding the bed with metal strips buried 10 cm (4 in) deep in the soil. For small gardens a few runners can be planted in a bottomless container, but these will need to be replanted more frequently; otherwise they will become very overcrowded.

Mentha x *spicata* L.
Family LABIATAE

Culinary Use This is the mint most commonly used for the traditional English mint sauce served with roast lamb, made with finely chopped young leaves, vinegar and sugar. If the strong flavour of malt vinegar is disliked, mint sauce made with wine or cider vinegar is much milder. In addition to its well known use with lamb, new potatoes and green peas, mint is very good cooked with carrots, courgettes and marrows, and added to marinades and vegetable salads. An unusual and delicious filling for a pasty, taken from an old recipe, can be made with equal quantities of chopped mint, currants and demerara sugar, moistened with a little apple or apricot purée and a knob of butter.

Mint dries successfully, either as whole leaves or crumbled, and retains its flavour well if kept in an airtight jar.

'Bowles Mint' (Hybrid)

This mint is thought to be a hybrid between *M. x spicata* and *M. sauveolens*. It is named after the well known plantsman E. A. Bowles (d 1954), who considered it to be the finest flavoured mint for culinary use. It is a vigorous plant which grows 60–120 cm (2–4 ft) tall and has sturdy underground and overground runners. The strong stems carry pairs of large, woolly, sessile, almost round leaves, 7·5 × 4·5 cm (3 × 1¾in). Pale lilac flowers are borne in long, dense terminal spikes. This is sometimes called round leaved, foxtail and woolly mint.

Cultivation Most people agree that 'Bowles mint' has a very fine flavour and it also has the advantage of being less susceptible to rust than garden mint, but it is of no commercial value as it wilts very rapidly when cut. This mint can be grown in a sunny position and will tolerate dry soils. It is a rampant grower, and unless its roots are confined it may overrun the whole border; these roots are brittle and not easy to eradicate. 'Bowles mint' is sufficiently vigorous to be grown in rough grass and, thus sheltered, will provide a supply of young shoots for use in the kitchen late into the autumn when the spearmint has died down. In the latter half of the summer the flower spikes will begin to form and the leaves will become leathery and the aroma less attractive. If the plants are cut back to three or four nodes they will send up a supply of fresh young growth suitable for use in the kitchen.

Mentha x *villosa alopecuroides*
Family LABIATAE

Culinary Use 'Bowles mint' is used in the same way as garden mint – the woolly texture of the leaves disappears when it is finely chopped and the full flavour is very good for mint sauce. It also dries well and retains its flavour for a long period so that it can be available throughout the winter. If dried mint is to be used for flavouring vegetables such as potatoes, carrots and stored marrows, and removed before serving, the leaves should be kept whole after drying instead of being crumbled.

This mint is sometimes mistakenly called apple mint, but the latter is another much smaller mint, also with woolly sessile leaves but far less vigorous, rarely growing more than 45 cm (18 in) tall and inferior to 'Bowles mint' in flavour. A variegated form of apple mint, well marked with bold splashes of creamy white and with some shoots entirely white, is a most decorative plant and is in great demand for flower arrangements. But it has very little flavour.

Eau de Cologne Mint

Mentha x *piperita citrata* L.
Family LABIATAE

This mint is considered to be a hybrid of *M. aquatica* and *M.* x *spicata*. There are several scented leaved mints which are very similar in appearance but not identical; these are bergamot mint, lemon mint and orange mint. They resemble each other closely and it is difficult to distinguish them unless they are all at hand at the same time. Eau de Cologne mint is generally considered the finest both in fragrance and appearance. It has stout, square stems, much branched towards the top, growing 30–45 cm (12–18 in) high. These upper branches are well clothed with pairs of thin, ovate-elliptical, petiolate smooth leaves, approximately 4 × 2·5 cm (1½ × 1 in) and terminate in flowering spikes with blue-purple flowers growing in dense whorls at well spaced intervals. The numerous and invasive runners are like bright purple ribbons lying over the soil.

Cultivation On fertile, moist soils the plant is tall and the leaves have a purplish tinge at the margins; if grown on exceptionally well drained soils the purplish flush covers the whole leaf, the stem is short, dark purple, and the aroma is far stronger. On alkaline soils the whole plant is finer and the flower colour deepens; the overground runners also are a deep rich purple. As with all mints, frequent replanting is necessary.

Culinary Use   Eau de Cologne mint is not commonly used as a culinary herb, but if a small sprig is included when garden mint is being used it will enhance the flavour. Some enthusiastic herb users like a mint sauce made entirely with this mint with roast pork; it is, however, stronger in flavour than garden mint. A refreshing summer drink can be made by infusing leaves in boiling water and sweetening it with honey for serving iced.

Other Uses   A bunch of Eau de Cologne mint will scent a linen cupboard, and the dried leaves added to pot-pourri or made into sachets for putting into drawers will provide a long lasting fragrance.

The long flower stems with their dense whorls of lilac-purple flowers last well in water and are very decorative, and they are frequently used in flower arrangements.

Peppermint

Although this mint is thought to have been known to the ancient Egyptians, and also to the Greeks and Romans, it was not given the English name of peppermint until the late seventeenth century by a British botanist, John Ray (1627–1715). He is famous as being the first to classify the flowering plants into monocotyledons and dicotyledons. In relatively few years after he had described and named the plant it was included in the official lists of medicinal herbs, the Pharmacopeias. Now it is widely grown on a commercial scale.

There are several varieties of peppermints; these are divided into two main groups, the black and the white. The varieties in the black group are robust plants mostly growing 60–75 cm (2–$2\frac{1}{2}$ ft) tall, and their stout purple stems are hairy and branched at the top. The thick, purple-flushed, stalked leaves are ovate-lanceolate, and are coarsely toothed and hairy on the underside and dotted with oil glands. The reddish-lilac flowers are in loose conical terminal spikes 4–7 cm ($1\frac{1}{2}$–$2\frac{1}{2}$ in) long. The white peppermints are slender plants, often shorter than the black, and are a cool green sometimes flushed with red. The white flowers are also tinged with red. The aroma of the varieties in this group is considerably milder and the oil derived from them is of a higher quality and commands a higher price.

Mentha x *piperita* L.
(Hybrid of *M. aquatica* L. x *M. spicata* L.)
Family LABIATAE

white

black

The large scale commercial industry for the production of oils from many herbs, including the peppermints, started in the late eighteenth century. The chief centres in the British Isles were Mitcham in Surrey, Market Deeping in Lincolnshire and Hitchin in Hertfordshire. The moist English climate is believed to account for the high quality of the oils obtained from plants grown on English farms as compared with the products of plants grown in countries with a hotter climate. The commercial production of peppermint oil is now almost world-wide, the most important producers being a number of European countries, the USSR, North and East Africa, Australia, China and Japan, and the United States, which produces the largest quantity.

Cultivation   A friable moist soil is essential, with the addition of well decayed compost or manure, and an open situation without too much shade is required. As the plants are hybrids they must be propagated by vegetative means, and strong healthy stolons should be planted 5 cm (2 in) deep and 30 cm (1 ft) apart in autumn. After 3–4 years plants will need to be dug up, divided and replanted.

Uses The tips of the plants are processed to obtain the peppermint oil, and the finest oil is obtained from the flowers just as they are beginning to open. The oil is extensively used in a great variety of ways, especially in medicines for the treatment of flatulence and coughs and colds, and in tonics to stimulate the appetite. It is also used in ointments for the relief of rheumatic pain. A home-made cure for indigestion and a stimulating beverage is made by infusing a handful of leaves in boiling water for five minutes; it is important to use only a china or pottery container for this. Oil of peppermint is used in toothpaste and cosmetics, and in confectionery.

This mint is sometime used in the kitchen instead of garden mint for adding to vegetables and for giving additional flavour to fruit cocktails and cream cheese spreads.

Pennyroyal

Mentha pulegium L.
(syn *Pulegium vulgare*)
Family LABIATAE

This small evergreen plant with a very strong odour of menthol is a native of most of Europe except the north, and has spread into North Africa and western Asia. It has a straggling, branching habit and may be prostrate, when it will root freely at nodes in contact with the soil, or it may scramble amongst nearby plants. The stems can grow as long as 45 cm (1½ ft). The fresh green leaves, 1–2 cm (½ in) long, may be oval or oblong, shallowly toothed or entire, and are short stalked. The flower stems are generally upright with numerous compact and globular widely spaced whorls of lilac flowers.

Cultivation This plant, which looks so fragile, withstands hot sunshine, cold and wet with impunity and grows strongly in sun or shade. It can be used as ground cover or for making a small path, and can be trodden with little damage, but as it is a very pale green it is not so suitable for a turf as the very similar species *Hedeoma pulegioides* from America. This latter plant is dark green and will make a denser turf. A path turfed with either of these pennyroyals is delightful to tread on, giving off a refreshing aroma of menthol, but it is unlikely to stand up to very hard wear. For instructions on using them for making a turf see page 24.

Uses Owing to its very pungent aroma, pennyroyal has almost no culinary value, although it has been used in country districts for flavouring soups and stews. In the past it was widely used both as a curative and as a household herb. The early apothecaries prescribed it for a great variety of ailments, including dropsy, gout and rheumatism, headaches, jaundice, stomach upsets and toothache, and for clearing the complexion. Pennyroyal was also thought to relieve depression and a bunch would be hung in a bedroom for this reason. In the days of sailing ships it was used to sweeten the drinking water. The specific name *pulegium* is derived from *pulex*, the Latin name for a flea, and pennyroyal was known to repel these pests; for this reason it was widely used as a strewing herb. The oil obtained from it is used in the present day as a repellant for gnats and mosquitoes, and a bunch hung up in the house helps to keep insects away.

In the eighteenth century this herb was cultivated on a commercial scale for the menthol content of its essential oil, and it still has some uses in herbal medicine.

Another interesting menthol-scented mint to grow is *Mentha requienii*. This is a minute plant, but it makes its presence known by a strong aroma reminiscent of chewing gum. It comes from Corsica and is commonly called the Corsican mint. During the summer months, if kept shaded, it spreads rapidly and forms a dense carpet, the stems rooting as they grow. It is a fresh light green and the rounded leaves 2–3 mm ($\frac{1}{10}$ in) in diameter overlap; the tiny lilac coloured flowers are in whorls in the leaf axils. During the winter *M. requienii* tends to die out and only minute scraps of growth can be found, but in most years by late summer there will be a fresh mossy carpet of foliage. It would appear that regeneration is from self sown seed.

No use is made of this tiny herb but it is interesting to add to a collection of this genus.

Nasturtium

Tropaeolum majus L.
Family TROPAEOLACEAE

This familiar plant, grown mainly for its gay flowers, is perennial in South America and was introduced into England from Peru in the sixteenth century. In temperate climates it must be treated as an annual. There are several forms; some are vigorous climbers, others make densely branching cushions, and some are dwarf and make small upright plants about 15 cm (6 in) tall. The round peltate leaves are usually light green, although in some varieties they are almost chocolate brown. They are most commonly 6–10 cm (2½–4 in) in diameter, with entire margins and long petioles. The flowers, 5–8 cm (2–3 in) in diameter, in various shades of cream, maroon, orange, scarlet and yellow, have five rounded petals and a long, curved nectar spur. The fruits consist of three joined fleshy seeds with conspicuous ribs.

Cultivation   A light soil in a sunny place is best for nasturtiums, but they will tolerate a shady place providing the drainage is good. They are very useful for maintaining a continuous supply of gaily coloured flowers throughout the summer. The seed is sown in late spring where the plants are to grow. Dwarf forms will be suitable for the front of the herb border but climbing forms are useful to make a colourful display on a trellis at the back.

Culinary Use   Leaves, flowers and seeds can be used in the kitchen. They have a hot peppery taste and contain vitamin C; the greatest concentration is in the leaves just before flowering. Chopped young leaves can be added to sandwich fillings and also to cream cheese – 2 teaspoonfuls to 100 g ($3\frac{1}{2}$ oz) – but this must be eaten while fresh as a bitter taste will develop with keeping. Young flowers add colour to a green salad, and the unripe seeds can be pickled in vinegar as a substitute for capers. The leaves dry well for winter use, and the ripened seeds can be dried and ground in a pepper mill for use as a seasoning.

Other Uses   Nasturtiums are cultivated commercially for the seed, which is gathered when ripe. An antibiotic is obtained from the dried and crushed seed which is used in the treatment of bronchitis and influenza, and for inflammation of the urinary passages. In herbal cures both leaves and flowers are used for their antiseptic and tonic properties, to improve the digestion, to cure constipation and to clear the skin, and they are also considered to be a valuable antidote for nervous depression. They are nutritious and are useful in diets in which salt and other seasonings have to be restricted or eliminated. Small doses taken daily are safer than large amounts. If taken in excess nasturtiums can be harmful and not more than 15 g ($\frac{1}{2}$ oz) should be eaten at any one time. Hot poultices made from the leaves are effective in the treatment of abscesses and skin troubles.

Iris germanica var *florentina* Dykes
Family IRIDACEAE

This iris is included here because the violet fragrance obtained from its rhizomes is particularly valued in the perfumery industry and in the manufacture of various household products. It is a native of southern Europe and is commonly seen growing in Italy. The orris root iris is one of the large rhizomatous group and resembles closely the many species and hybrids known as flag or German irises so frequently seen in many gardens. *I. g.* var *florentina* is perennial, with stouter fleshy rhizomes than those of the majority of this group. It has attractive sword shaped leaves 50 cm (1½ ft) long and 4 cm (1½ in) wide and covered with a whitish bloom. The flowering stems which arise annually from the rhizomes in late spring or early summer may be 60 cm (2 ft) tall and terminate in two or three large, almost stalkless flowers enclosed in a scarious-edged sheaf. They are white, feathered with bluish purple and have conspicuous beards on the three outer petals. The two closely related species *I. g. f. albicans*, (white and beardless), and *I. pallida*, a taller plant with delightful pale blue flowers with yellow beards arising from a scarious sheath, are also used for the production of orris root.

In Italy these rhizomatous irises are frequently to be seen clinging to the stony edges of high banks on roadsides, railway cuttings, etc, where they have perfect drainage with full exposure to sun. These conditions, however, are too harsh for the full development of the required fleshy rhizomes, and the irises grown as a commercial crop will be seen on the more fertile upland soils.

Cultivation   These three beautiful irises introduce colour and bring interest to the herb border, where most of the plants have only rather small and insignificant flowers. Well decayed compost should be dug into the site where they are to grow. In planting the rhizomes are placed 15 cm (6 in) apart and must be kept on the surface of the soil. The previous season's roots are spread out horizontally and firmly buried in shallow holes at either side of the rhizomes. The flowering period is May and early June. After the flowers have faded the flower stems are cut back, and great care must be taken not to damage the leaves. These must continue to grow throughout the summer season to build up the rhizome for the following year. Three or four years after planting the rhizomes will have multiplied considerably and will be crowded and matted. They should then be lifted, divided and replanted. This is best done four to five weeks after the flowers have died. After lifting, the more robust rhizomes should be selected. The roots, which are annual in duration, will be mainly dead and must be shortened, leaving 6 cm (2 in); this will be sufficient to anchor the replanted rhizomes to the soil. They should be replanted as indicated above; do not be tempted to plant too thickly. In a very short time the new season's roots will begin to grow on the rhizomes.

If it is impossible to replant in late June before the new roots grow, the work may be carried out in early autumn or in mid spring. By then the new feeding roots will be well developed and must be handled with great care; if they are injured the plants may not flower the following season. With careful handling, and with watering if the weather is dry, flowering will not be affected.

Uses   To produce orris root the harvested rhizomes are washed, dried thoroughly and crushed to a fine powder to release the violet scented oil from the plant tissue. The oil is used in perfumery and the powder as a fixative in pot-pourri, and both are ingredients of many cosmetics and household products. In former times orris root was used medicinally for a variety of ailments, especially chest complaints, and as a purgative, and the dried root was given to babies when teething. It had serious side effects, however, and is no longer used for internal medicines.

Garden Parsley

Petroselinum crispum Mill.
Family UMBELLIFERAE

This plant is native to central and southern Europe and is a biennial or a short lived perennial. It has a stout tap root and triangular, deeply cut leaves. In the species the leaves are uncurled and have a stronger flavour than garden parsley, but this plain leaved plant is seldom grown as it may easily be confused with the highly poisonous fool's parsley, *Aethusa cynapium*. Most gardeners choose to grow one of the varieties which have curled leaves. Some of these are so excessively curled, however, that they tend to rot in prolonged wet weather, and they also vary in the intensity of their green colour. In the second year after seed sowing the solid, branching stems 60 cm (2 ft) tall carry compound umbels of small greenish-yellow flowers, and the brown seeds are conspicuously ribbed. Roots, stems, leaves and seeds are all aromatic.

Cultivation Parsley should be grown on fertile, moist, deeply cultivated soil and is most successful in positions which are shaded during the hottest part of the day. It is propagated by seed sown in spring, but as cold soil inhibits germination sowing should be delayed until the soil has warmed. If the drills are sown and then partially covered with soil, and boiling water is poured over them before they are completely filled in, germination will be accelerated. It is not usual to transplant parsley seedlings, but this can be done successfully provided they are very small. If the roots of the seedlings are well developed they may be damaged by transplantation, and this will make them likely to bolt. It has long been said that transplanting parsley is not possible, but this is probably due to an old superstition that if it is transplanted a disaster to the household will follow. Thinning is essential to obtain strong plants which will come through the winter. Crowded plants are more liable to damage during cold wet spells. In cold areas it may be advisable to cover the plants with well ventilated cloches during frosty periods, or to maintain a winter supply by keeping a pot on a windowsill. Some seedsmen list dwarf varieties which are particularly successful for growing indoors; one of these is 'Clivi'. As with many biennial plants, the life of parsley can be lengthened by one or two years if it is not allowed to flower and seed. On the other hand, self sown seedlings will keep up the supply and thus make further planned sowing unnecessary unless the winter is unusually wet and cold.

Culinary Use Parsley is rich in vitamins A, B and C and also in the minerals calcium, iron, magnesium and sodium, and it should be eaten and not used merely as a garnish. The stems, which have the most flavour, are always included in a *bouquet garni*. When parsley is used in a cooked dish it should always be added towards the end of the cooking period to preserve the vitamin content and green colour. Chopped leaves are added to soups, sauces, omelettes and scrambled eggs and sprinkled over salads and cooked vegetables. It is the main ingredient of dried mixed herbs, and if it is dried fairly quickly it will retain its bright green colour.

Other Uses Roots, stems, leaves and seeds all contain a medicinally valuable essential oil, but parsley should be taken as a herbal cure only with professional advice as too great a concentration of apiol, a constituent of the oil, may have a harmful effect. It is used mainly for various digestive disorders. It stimulates the appetite and is a remedy for flatulence. A green dye is obtained from the stems.

Rosemary

Rosemary is a native of the Mediterranean coast. Its name derives from early Latin and means 'sea dew'. It is a much branched evergreen shrub growing approximately 1 m (3 ft) high; the main wood quickly becomes rough, with loose strips of bark giving the plant a rugged appearance. Young plants are dense with closely packed shoots, but with age soon become open and sparse. The linear leaves are deep green and leathery; they are 3 cm (1 in) long and 2 mm ($\frac{1}{10}$ in) wide and are tomentose below with revolute margins. The small stemless flowers, generally grey blue, with prominent lower lobes, are in short racemes in the leaf axils. A form coming from Corsica, *R. o. angustifolia*, with narrower and shorter leaves and rich blue flowers, has a much more pungent aroma.

There are several named forms of the common rosemary. 'Miss Jessup's Upright' has a compact habit and grows 2 m (6 ft 6 in) high. 'Tuscan Blue' has a broader leaf, and 'Seven Seas' is lower growing with spreading branches; both have deeper blue flowers and are more attractive than the common form with its pale grey-blue flowers.

Rosmarinus officinalis L.
Family LABIATAE

Cultivation This shrub, requiring sun and excellent drainage, is best grown in the shelter of a wall. When grown in the open garden it is often damaged by the winter gales. Young and vigorous plants will withstand severe winter conditions better than gaunt, woody bushes, and once the plants have become straggling they should be replaced. This is usually necessary after 5–6 years. Careful pruning will help to keep the growth compact, but branches should never be cut back into bare wood. Propagation is simple as short woody shoots removed from the parent plant in summer will root easily in sandy soil in the open.

R. o. angustifolia will make a compact bush if long shoots are continuously cut back to within 10–15 cm (4–6 in) of the roots. It is most conspicuous in flower and continues to bloom throughout the summer.

Culinary Use Rosemary is a useful kitchen herb, but only young leaves should be used and these are usually removed before serving. Soft young sprigs laced into the skin of a joint of lamb or of a chicken before roasting impart a very appetising flavour, and sachets of rosemary leaves can be cooked with casseroles, old potatoes or spinach. This herb is also used in marinades and features largely in Greek and Italian cookery. It is one of the most strongly flavoured herbs, and care should be taken not to use it in excess.

Other Uses Rosemary was once considered to be of the utmost importance both for its curative properties and for the maintenance of good health, but it is now used only in herbal cures. The essential oil is thought to stimulate the appetite and aid digestion. It is also used in liniments and ointments for the relief of neuritis and rheumatism, and in bath oils, shampoos and soaps. The strong volatile oil is considered to be germicidal and insect repellant, and before disinfectants were readily available branches of this herb were burnt in sickrooms to purify the atmosphere.

It is by long tradition the 'herb of remembrance' and is called this by Ophelia in Shakespeare's *Hamlet*. Gilded branches of it were once carried at weddings, and it was customary to lay rosemary on the coffin at a funeral.

Ruta graveolens L.
Family RUTACEAE

Rue is an aromatic evergreen subshrub native to southern Europe and is found in sheltered places on well drained rocky soils, mostly in the limestone regions. It grows 45–80 cm (1½–2½ ft) tall, with a crowded growth of small shoots with doubly pinnate, rubbery textured leaves 3 × 3 cm (1¼ × 1¼ in). These curl downwards from long petioles and the undersides are dotted with small oil glands. The small yellow flowers with four concave petals grow in loose clusters at the ends of the shoots. Rue has a curious, cloying, sweetish aroma, difficult to define.

Cultivation On well drained soils this decorative evergreen shrub is generally unharmed by low temperatures, and thus is particularly valuable in the winter garden. It should be grown in a sunny open place to encourage robust and hardy growth. To maintain the dense cushion-like habit which is more attractive than the naturally sprawling open bush the plant should be lightly clipped with shears just as growth commences in spring. The insignificant dull yellow flowers detract from the appearance of the blue-grey foliage and should be removed by clipping as soon as they appear.

As rue is generally grown as a decorative feature in the herb garden, the variety 'Jackman's Blue' which has larger and bluer leaves than the type is a good form to choose. There is also a variegated variety which has specks of yellow in the leaves.

Rue is easy to propagate. A well ripened shoot with a heel removed from the shrub in late summer and inserted in sandy soil in a sunny place in the open will usually form roots by the following spring.

Culinary Use　It is unusual for this bitter tasting herb to be used in food in modern times, although some people find it agreeable when finely chopped and added to sandwich fillings or sprinkled over a salad. It should always be used with great restraint.

Other Uses　Rue was widely used in medicine in ancient Greece, and was probably brought to northern Europe by the Romans. Among its many uses in the past it was employed as an antidote to poisons, for arresting haemorrhage and reducing inflammation. It was also used to remove warts. A lotion made from the herb was used in the treatment of eye strain, and a chewed leaf was believed to ease the tension causing headaches.

It is still used in medicine to a limited extent, chiefly in the treatment of nervous disorders, but as excessive doses can be toxic it should be taken only under medical supervision.

Rue, known as the 'herb of grace', was used to sprinkle holy water before the celebration of High Mass. It was a symbol of regret and remembrance. Ophelia refers to this in *Hamlet*. With rosemary, it was long esteemed as a protection against pests and diseases and both were used as nosegays to be carried before the presiding judges in the Old Bailey, to ward off the fleas and lice brought in by the prisoners from the pestilence-ridden jails. This custom is still preserved as a tradition.

Sage

The common sage is native to southern Europe and is found on the south-facing slopes of the limestone uplands in full sun. It is an evergreen shrub, approximately 75 cm (2½ ft) tall, with a dense growth of twigs and foliage arising from the stout, woody main stem and branches. The heavily veined, grey-green, felted leaves with finely serrated margins are 5 × 2 cm (2 × ¾ in), with long petioles. In early summer the handsome spikes of blue-purple flowers, 15–20 cm (6–8 in) long, appear. This sage is one of the most pungent herbs.

Salvia officinalis L.
Family LABIATAE

golden

purple

tricolor

Cultivation   Full sun and good drainage are essential for this strongly aromatic herb. Unless it is closely trimmed after flowering the bush will become gaunt and open, and liable to be damaged by wind and heavy snowfalls. The 15 cm (6 in) long flower spikes terminate the annual growth, and as the flowers fade these spikes must be clipped hard back. Where a high yield of sage is important the flowerless form known as 'English broad leaf' is grown. There are several coloured leaf forms of *S. officinalis*; all make low spreading bushes without the woody leg of the common sage. The golden sage, *S. o.* 'Icterina', has yellow bands of colour in the leaf which deepen as the summer progresses, so that by the autumn the bush appears completely golden.

The tricolor sage, *S. o.* 'Tricolor', varies greatly in colour; some forms are splashed with silver, purple and green and some with pink and yellow. Neither of these is so robust and hardy as the purple sage, *S. o.* 'Purpurascens' which makes a very vigorous and spreading cushion of growth. All are highly decorative plants suitable for the front of the border, but they need to be renewed more frequently than the common sage. They may all be used in the kitchen and have a milder flavour.

Sage must never be cut back below the young growth as the bare old wood will not produce new buds, even with careful pruning. After 4–5 years sage bushes become sprawling and untidy and need to be replaced. Cuttings with woody ends will root easily if put into sandy soil in a shady place during the summer months.

Culinary Use   Like most of the highly aromatic herbs sage has long been used to flavour food and wine, and is used commercially in the processing of foods. Although its strong flavour is not popular with everyone it is widely used in stuffing for rich meat and poultry, and in pork sausages, meat loaves and certain hard and soft cheeses, eg, sage derby cheese with its flecks of green. As an alternative, whole leaves may be placed on roasting joints or grills of pork or veal or on liver for braising, and when treated in this way only a little of the pungent oil is released from the leaf.

Other Uses   Traditionally sage is held to be the herb for the promotion of good health. The generic name is derived from the Latin *salvere*, meaning 'to save'. The essential oil distilled from the dried leaves is used in medicine largely as an antibiotic. From early times it has been used as a cure for a vast number of ailments and it was a common saying that 'He who would live for aye must eat sage in May'. It is now used as an ingredient of medicines for digestive troubles, loss of appetite, biliousness and liver complaints, headaches and nervous troubles. The Chinese were said to value sage so highly that they once bartered their own teas for sage tea from the West.

In the past sage leaves were burnt as a deodorizer, and sage oil is used in the present day in soaps and perfumery.

Salad Burnet

Sanguisorba minor Scop.
Family ROSACEAE

This small perennial herb with a woody rootstock is native to Europe and Asia and is found mainly on dry chalky soils. It has a tufted rosette of fresh green pinnate leaves approximately 15×3 cm ($6 \times 1\frac{1}{4}$ in) with round and toothed leaflets, resembling a bunch of feathers. The small globular heads of flowers on branched stems are light green when they first appear and turn a reddish brown after pollination. These heads contain many tiny flowers, and in this species the flowers at the lower half are male, with many stamens which can be seen hanging down in tufts, the flowers in the centre are bisexual, and the uppermost flowers are female with long styles ending in feathery stigmas.

Another much larger species is *Sanguisorba officinalis*, commonly called the great burnet; this has similar though much larger globular flower heads but all the tiny flowers are bisexual. Owing to this difference in the flower characteristics some botanists have put salad burnet into a separate species and in certain reference books it will be found as *Poterium sanguisorba L.*

Cultivation Although salad burnet is not widely grown in the present day it is an attractive plant to include in the herb garden,

especially as the delightfully dainty foliage will survive the winter. It will grow in sun or shade and on any soil. In Elizabethan times *S. minor* was known as God's little birds, the name referring to the small upstanding leaves on the fine stems. Francis Bacon, in his essay 'On Gardens' recommends using it in alleys with wild thyme and water mint 'to have the pleasure when you walk or tread'; the fragrance of the bruised leaves, like that of chamomile and pennyroyal, is very refreshing, particularly in the evening.

Uses In the time of Bacon young leaves of this herb were put into wine 'to refresh the spirits', and it was used in many herbal cures, for treating diarrhoea and haemorrhoids and various other ailments. It is not longer included in the official pharmocopeia.

In modern usage the addition of young leaves to salads for their cool and nutty flavour is recommended, and they are also used in asparagus and mushroom soups and sauces. These young leaves put into wine and cider cups will add a flavour akin to that of cucumber.

In herbal medicines a tea is prepared from the dried roots which is recommended as a cure for dysentery, and it is said that chewing a leaf will assist the digestion.

Summer Savory

This is a bushy little annual 15–35 cm (6–14 in) in height, native to southeast Europe and southwest Asia on dry limestone soils. It seeds freely and is now widespread as a garden escape. It is a much branched, erect growing small bush; the oblong linear leaves are rarely larger than 15 × 2 mm ($\frac{1}{2}$ × $\frac{1}{10}$ in), and the whole plant is pubescent and slightly rough to handle. Both stems and leaves may be green or deep purple, and the showy little flowers in the leaf axils are a bright pinkish purple. Both leaves and calyx are heavily dotted with glands in which the essential oil is stored.

Cultivation Summer savory grows well on all soils and does not appear to be affected by wet winters. Sow the seed direct where the plants are to grow in late spring; if cold weather persists cover with cloches, and thin the seedlings when large enough to 15 cm (6 in) apart.

The plants branch freely from the central stem and by late July flowers appear in every leaf axil. Once summer savory has been grown in the garden self sown seedlings will be found wherever it has been growing in previous years. Although it appears to be a fragile little annual the seedlings can easily be transplanted. It is said that if summer savory is grown amongst broad beans the crop will not be infested with black fly. For this the seed must be sown early in a seed box and seedlings transplanted fairly thickly in between the bean plants; otherwise they will be too small to provide the effective protection.

Satureja hortensis L.
Family LABIATAE

Culinary Use   The flowering leafy shoots can be used fresh or dried in a great variety of foods. The herb has a delicious flavour, both peppery and aromatic, and it reduces the need for pepper. It helps to make foods such as beans, cucumbers, lentils and raw vegetable salads more easily digested, and is added to baked fish, sausages, stuffings, patés and pork pies; it is particularly recommended for omelettes. In Germany it is cooked with all kinds of beans and known as *bohnenkraut*, the 'bean herb'. When beans are being prepared for deep freezing small bunches of summer savory may be included in the packs and will greatly improve the flavour when they are cooked. The unpleasant odour which arises during the cooking of the various brassicas disappears if this herb is cooked with them. All uncooked vegetable salads are greatly improved in flavour by the addition of the freshly chopped leaves. The annual summer savory has a more delicate flavour than the shrubby winter savory, but because of its pungency the latter is more usually included in dried herb mixtures.

Other Uses   The dried flowering shoots are used in herbal remedies for the treatment of gastric complaints and as an aid to digestion, and the essential oil extracted from the herb is used in the preparation of foods in the canning industry.

Winter Savory

This is a small subshrub which comes from southeast Europe and North Africa and can be found on dry chalk soils and rocky mountain slopes. With its markedly silvery basal wood and twiggy habit, it is very different in appearance from the annual summer savory. If left unpruned the plant grows approximately 30 cm (1 ft) tall, with greyish branching stems and sessile oblong linear leaves which are light green and leathery, $2 \cdot 5 \times 5$ mm ($1 \times \frac{1}{5}$in). These leaves are sharply pointed, and this and the pale colour distinguishes the winter savory in spring and early summer from the rather similar hyssop, which has deep green blunt-ended leaves. The loose clusters of pale pinkish flowers appear in late summer in the axils of the current season's growth.

Cultivation   Unlike summer savory which is found on the fringes of cultivated land and in meadows, this small easily grown shrub coming from barren mountain slopes needs poor and well drained soil. If grown on a damp, rich soil it is liable to be killed in a severe winter. When grown for use in the kitchen it must be cut back each year to 3–6 cm ($1\frac{1}{4}$–$2\frac{1}{2}$ in) of the woody rootstock to encourage the growth of the tender, upright leafy stems which will be required. If not pruned it makes a small wiry plant. It is a useful plant for the front of the herb

Satureja montana L.
Family LABIATAE

border, and as it continues to flower late into the autumn it is often planted in a rock garden. A creeping form, *S. m. subspicata*, is often selected for this purpose. As winter savory is perennial it is less trouble to grow than the annual summer savory, although once sown the latter will re-appear each year from self sown seed in any soil left undisturbed. Winter savory is easily propagated by division in spring. Both savories are very attractive to bees.

Culinary Use   This herb is too pungent for most people's taste when used on its own, but it is the savory which is used in dried herb mixtures, when a particularly spicy and peppery flavour is required. As the leaves tend to become very hard when dried they should be well pulverized before use. The fresh young leaves can be used to replace summer savory in any dish, but always in very small amounts only.

Other Uses   Winter savory is used in herbal medicine as a digestant, and as a seasoning in the food industry. One particular use for it is in Italian charcuterie such as salami.

Saponaria officinalis L.
Family CARYOPHYLLACEAE

POISONOUS

This is another plant which is included in collections of herbs mainly for its historical associations, although it also has an important modern use. The genus is widespread throughout Europe and southern Asia. It is closely allied to the genus *Dianthus*, and *S. officinalis* is not unlike the sweet william grown in gardens. In fact, one of its common names is wild sweet william, but it is perennial and has softer and more sprawling growth. It is commonly to be seen in late summer growing in spreading masses on the wide verges of the main roads in northern France. The underground portion of the plant is a tangled mass of stem-like scaly rhizomes. The annual shoots are sturdy and erect, about 30 cm (1 ft) tall, with pairs of elliptical-shaped leaves 5–7 cm (2–3 in) long with conspicuous parallel veining and short, broad, stem-clasping petioles. The stems terminate in dense corymbs of white or pale pink flowers, each 1·5 cm (¾ in) wide. This plant is found in great quantity on the coasts of Devon and Cornwall and may be indigenous.

Cultivation   The double flowered form is generally chosen for planting in the garden; it is more suitable for the informal type of garden. It would be an unwise choice unless the roots could be restricted, but it is a useful plant to put into corners where little else but weeds will grow. It flourishes in well drained soil in a sunny place, but must never be planted in the vicinity of a pool containing fish or other aquatic animals as it has toxic properties. The plant contains saponin which is a poison and water draining from the roots or debris from the leaves could be fatal to them. In fact, the plant was once used as a fish poison.

Uses   There are references to the use of *Saponaria* as a cleansing agent in the writings of Dioscorides, who lived in the first century and was a surgeon in Nero's army. His major work, *De Materia Medica* was the standard work on healing plants during the succeeding fifteen hundred years. The generic name is derived from the Latin *sapo*, meaning 'soap' and is an indication of its use. It will lather in water like soap and has been used for centuries to clean and restore the colours of delicate fabrics such as old carpets or tapestries. It is mild in action and there is no risk when it is used in the correct solution. This is made by boiling 50 g ($1\frac{3}{4}$ oz) of roots in 1 litre ($1\frac{3}{4}$ pints) of water for ten minutes. After straining, the liquid is applied gently with a sponge or soft cloth. This preparation is used by the National Trust when restoring the famous collections of needlework in the great houses in its care. It should be remembered that the glycocide saponin is toxic and needs to be handled with care. Gloves should be worn when handling the solution.

Soapwort has little medicinal use, but since medieval times both roots and leaves have been used in the treatment of skin complaints, jaundice and venereal disease. In some instances, however, even very small doses have been known to have adverse side effects such as severe inflammation, and the drug must be specially treated before it is used and only administered by a qualified medical practitioner.

Other common names of this plant are latherwort, bruisewort and bouncing Bet.

French Sorrel
Garden Sorrel

Rumex scutatus L.
Family POLYGONACEAE

Two species of *Rumex* are used for culinary purposes, the broad leaved form of common sorrel, *R. acetosa*, and French sorrel, *R. scutatus*, with its decorative, shield-like silvery leaves.

French sorrel is found throughout the southern regions of Europe and Asia. It is a striking plant which makes a low hummock of lax stems about 30 cm (12 in) high. The long-stalked leaves, approximately 6 × 7 cm ($2\frac{1}{2}$ × $2\frac{3}{4}$ in), are hastate and greyish green with distinctive silvery markings. The stems terminate in slender branching spikes of scattered, reddish flowers which appear in mid to late summer.

Cultivation A sheltered position in full sun with good drainage is necessary for *R. scutatus*. In this situation the numerous slender stems make a compact cushion of growth. The greyish leaves, shaped like blunt arrow-heads, develop their silvery markings more fully when exposed to bright sunlight. Vigorously growing plants will yield the best leaves for culinary purposes, and lifting and dividing should be carried out every four to five years. The reddish, brittle roots look like a tangle of thick string. As broken root fragments left in the soil readily form new plants there is no problem of propagation, but these need to be completely cleared from the ground when the bed is being remade.

Garden sorrel is a broad leaved form of *R. acetosa*, the common sorrel, a widespread weed throughout Europe and Asia on all moist fertile soils. The leaves are oblong, sagittate at the base and tapering to a blunt apex; they are a fresh green colour suffused with reddish-brown, and may be 15 cm (6 in) across at their widest point, and 25 cm (10 in) long, with a long petiole. The erect, branched inflorescence has leafless panicles of reddish, unisexual flowers. The plant may be 60–90 cm (24–36 in) tall when flowering. Garden sorrel is similar in appearance to the dock but it is taller and the leaves are far wider and more succulent and an attractive fresh green.

Some confusion in identity has arisen as this broad leaved common sorrel has also been known as French sorrel.

Rumex acetosa L.
Family POLYGONACEAE

Cultivation A sheltered position in full sun and moist soil are best for garden sorrel. Young leaves only are required for culinary use, and these can be provided by frequent division or by seed. To maintain a season's supply flowering must be prevented, but if seed is to be saved for future crops one flower spike should be allowed to develop.

Culinary Use Sorrel leaves contain vitamin C and are recommended for purifying the blood, but they must be eaten with discretion as they contain oxalic acid which can be harmful to health if taken in excess. French sorrel is far less acid than garden sorrel and should be used by those who prefer to avoid acid foods. Young leaves chopped small may be added to scrambled eggs or omelettes just before serving, or sprinkled over green salads, and the sharp tangy flavour combines well with spinach. Sorrel also gives a piquant additional flavour to vegetable soups such as lentil, lettuce, spinach and watercress, although the sorrel soup and creamed sorrel which are much appreciated in France may not appeal to all tastes. Whole leaves of garden sorrel when bruised and wrapped round a joint of meat will act as a tenderizer.

Southernwood

This southern European subshrub with soft, fine, feathery grey-green foliage is to be seen in many gardens. Some consider its aroma to be pungent and rather unpleasant while others describe it as apple scented. The spikes of insignificant yellowish flowers are rarely seen in Great Britain owing to the short duration of summer heat. The current season's growth is usually cut back by cold weather in winter, leaving a twiggy bush of smooth brownish wood. Although at the present time *A. abrotanum* has only limited use as a herbal plant it is often included in the herb garden as a decorative feature, for it provides a useful contrast of form and foliage.

Cultivation Southernwood needs light soil and sun. Its ultimate height is controlled by yearly clipping. As new growth is appearing in spring the last year's growth should be cut back to 5–6 cm (2–$2\frac{1}{2}$ in) above its base; the numerous fresh shoots will quickly make an attractive dome-shaped hummock of new foliage. Unless this cutting back is done each year the untrimmed bush will become straggling and open.

Artemisia abrotanum L.
Family COMPOSITAE

Uses   During the time of the Roman Empire southernwood was used as a medicinal herb for its healing and fever reducing properties. A tonic was prepared from the leafy shoots, and bunches of these were added to bath water. The aromatic oil is still used today in bath preparations. This subshrub was introduced into England in Elizabethan times, when it was in great demand both as a medicinal and household herb. It was used to reduce menstrual pains and as a remedy for gastric troubles. Children were given it as a cure for worms; the dried and powdered foliage was mixed with treacle for this purpose. Several species of *Artemisia* have been used as vermicides and the name wormwood is loosely applied to all of them. In particular wormwood is the common name of *A. absinthium* (see page 137). Some of these species are native to northern Europe and would be well known to the countryfolk of the sixteenth and seventeenth centuries. Southernwood with its strong aroma was considered to be a valuable disinfectant and insect repellant and with many other strong smelling plants was used as a strewing herb on the bare uncarpeted floors.

The dried stems and leaves yield an essential oil known as absinthol, which has antiseptic and tonic properties and is now used in herbal preparations for gastric complaints. Extracts of young leaves are used in antiseptic detergents. The French name for this plant is *Garde robe*, an indication of its popular use; the dried herb is put into sachets to be hung in wardrobes to repel moths. The dried foliage may be used in pot-pourri, and a good yellow dye can be obtained from the stems and leaves. In spite of the strong flavour of southernwood it is used in some southern European countries as a kitchen herb.

Sweet Cicely

Myrrhis odorata L.
Family UMBELLIFERAE

This attractive herbaceous perennial is native to Europe. It tolerates a wide range of conditions and is found both in mountainous regions and in the lowlands. It has small, fleshy, swollen underground roots which are edible, and widely spreading, much divided and fernlike light green leaves 60 × 60 cm (24 × 24 in). These become noticeably flecked with white as the plant ages. The 70 cm (27 in) tall branched flower stems carry markedly flat umbels 10 cm (4 in) in diameter of creamy coloured flowers in early summer, followed by upstanding 2 cm ($\frac{3}{4}$ in) long oblong fruits; these become jet black on ripening.

Cultivation   This plant makes a very decorative feature in the herb garden with its pale lacy foliage and grows equally well in sun or shade providing the soil is moist. It is one of the earliest herb plants to come into growth in the spring, but in a very hot summer the growth may almost cease. It is easily grown and spreads rapidly both by small root tubers and by seeding, and on the heavier soils it will become very invasive unless kept in check by removing the seed before it is shed. The spreading plants are restrained by frequent dividing and replanting, or by replacing old plants by some of the small plants from root tubers which will be found in the vicinity.

Culinary Use   Sweet cicely has a sweet, sugary, mildly aniseed aroma. It is used as a sugar substitute by sufferers from diabetes. Finely chopped young leaves may be added to lettuce and vegetable salads, mixed into cream cheese, or sprinkled over omelettes, strawberries and trifles. The acidity of certain fruits such as black or red currants, gooseberries, plums or rhubarb is reduced by adding a few pieces of leaf stem or leaves, or by using dried leaves (2–3 teaspoonfuls to 454 g [1 lb] of fruit). As well as lessening the quantity of sugar required this herb gives an attractive flavour to the fruit. If the herb is used in highly seasoned dishes, however, the delicate flavour is lost. The small fleshy root tubers may also be used in the kitchen. They may be boiled and served cold with a light dressing of olive oil and lemon juice.

Other Uses   The anise flavouring obtained from sweet cicely is used in the making of the liqueur chartreuse.

The plant produces a rich brown dye useful in home dyeing.

Tarragon

This species of *Artemisia* is a native of southern Europe. It is an herbaceous perennial with a mass of fragile, fleshy roots from which a number of slender, upright, branching stems 90 cm (3 ft) tall appear yearly. These are clothed with fresh green, linear leaves 5 × 1 cm (2 × $\frac{1}{3}$ in), on the undersides of which can be seen the oil glands in which the aromatic essential oil is stored. When they are bruised a delicious peppery aroma is released. In late summer greenish-yellow balls of flowers appear in the upper shoots.

Artemisia dracunculus L.
Family LABIATAE

It is most important to obtain the well flavoured French tarragon when starting a herb garden. Another form, the Russian tarragon, growing 1·5 m (5 ft) tall, and with narrower and shorter greyish leaves, has a markedly less pleasant flavour and is not worth growing.

Cultivation The requirements are a friable soil with plenty of humus, good drainage and a sunny position. During the winter, in readiness for planting in spring, the site should be well prepared by digging the ground deeply to break up compacted sub-soil, to improve drainage; this will encourage the brittle roots of the plant to penetrate more deeply. Humus in the form of well decayed manure, garden compost, or horticultural peat, should be incorporated at this stage. If the soil is very heavy grit or small stones can be added as well to prevent compaction. Spring planting is recommended unless the young plants have been raised in pots. If planting is carried out in the autumn any injured roots may not have time to heal before the weather deteriorates and will probably decay in a cold wet winter. During dry periods in the summer months the plants should be well watered.

To maintain a vigorous stock tarragon plants should be lifted and divided every 3–4 years. When the new site has been enriched as previously described, only the vigorous growths from the edges of the original clump should be selected for replanting. This operation should

132

be carried out in the spring, just as the new growth is beginning to emerge. If left undisturbed and crowded for a number of years French tarragon deteriorates rapidly. The plant can only be propagated by vegetative means, but on light soils where it does not grow strongly lifting and dividing may be considered unwise. In this case new plants can be raised by removing shoots about 24 cm (9 in) long with a piece of root attached from the parent plant some time in May. These should be potted separately and protected with polythene bags until they are well rooted. By the autumn they will be strong young plants and can be transferred without root disturbance to a prepared position.

Culinary Use   Tarragon is pleasantly bitter-sweet and highly aromatic. It is generally used on its own and not with other herbs. It is particularly delicious with chicken, but has many other uses, with meat and fish, game, liver and kidneys, in sauces, soups, stuffings and salad dressings, and sprinkled over salads and cooked vegetables. Tarragon vinegar is made by steeping leafy shoots in wine or cider vinegar for at least fourteen days, and used for making continental mustards and tartare sauce.

Other Uses   Like the other artemisias tarragon was once used as an anthelmintic, ie, to expel internal worms. It is also used in the treatment of intestinal catarrh and as a stimulant for the appetite.

The specific name *dracunculus*, meaning 'a little dragon', is thought to be derived from an ancient use as an antidote to the bites of snakes and other venomous creatures.

Common Thyme

This little shrub, sometimes known as black thyme, is native to the Mediterranean regions and is found growing on dry soils and rocky slopes in sunny positions. It has very short, tough and woody stems, densely twiggy branch growth, and fine wiry annual shoots 3–5 cm (1–2 in) long. These shoots are clothed with pairs of small leathery leaves 5×2 mm ($\frac{1}{5} \times \frac{1}{12}$ in) with revolute margins. The small loose heads of pale lilac flowers appear in early summer. There are a number of forms of common thyme and these vary considerably both in appearance and aroma. The form known as French thyme has broader leaves and a sweeter and less pungent aroma than the common form.

Thymus vulgaris L.
Family LABIATAE

Cultivation   This is the thyme most commonly grown in gardens. An ideal position for it is a sloping bank of well drained soil in full sun, but if this is not available a bed of stony soil should be prepared. From the small woody head arises an annual growth of short leafy shoots which terminate in the flower clusters. As these fade the bushes should be clipped over with shears; this will encourage a new growth of shoots for the remainder of the summer. After this second crop has been gathered in early September the plants should again be trimmed with shears. After four or five years the plants become increasingly woody and less productive of young shoots for kitchen use and will need to be replaced by newly propagated stock. A simple method of obtaining young plants from the original stock is to fill the plant with well drained soil up to the base of the young wood. New roots will form on this wood and the plant can be lifted the following spring and the rooted growths separated and transplanted. This method is illustrated in Diagram 6 in the section on propagation. An alternative method of increase is by heel cuttings. The French thyme, which is considered to be superior, is a selected form of the common thyme and is unlikely to come true from seed.

   All the thymes are attractive to bees and should be planted freely near to the hives.

Culinary Use Common thyme is strongly flavoured and needs to be used sparingly. It is one of the herbs included in a *bouquet garni*, and also in dried mixed herbs. It can be used in any savoury dish and sprinkled over salads and vegetables. An unusual and delicious marinade for chicken portions consists of chopped fresh or dried thyme with olive oil, grated lemon rind and juice, a little garlic and freshly ground black pepper and salt. It must be stressed, however, that if thyme is used too lavishly its flavour will be overwhelming and will destroy the natural flavour of the food.

Other Uses The volatile oil of thymol, which is a well known and powerful disinfectant and germicide, is obtained from this species of thyme. A mixture of thymol and olive oils has long been recommended for use externally to relieve rheumatic pain. Infusions of the herb are used to aid digestion and stimulate the appetite, and also as a remedy for coughs and colds, bronchial complaints and intestinal disorders. Thymol oil is also used in surgical dressings, mouth washes and gargles, and in bath oils.

Lemon Thyme

This hybrid of *Thymus vulgaris* differs greatly in appearance from common thyme by its lack of woody growth at ground level, and by the thin, wiry spreading stems 10–15 cm (4–6 in) long, which bear the new season's growth. The leaves appear to be broader as the margins are not revolute as in common thyme, and the flowers are rose pink and more clustered and appear later in the summer. This thyme has a subtle lemony aroma.

T. herba-barona, the caraway-scented thyme from Corsica, is a low growing, spreading plant. The wiry shoots, 12 cm (5 in) long, arch, rooting into the ground at the tips and making a loose carpet of growth.

Cultivation Lemon thyme requires more care in the garden than the majority of herb plants; it dies out if conditions are unfavourable. It should be grown in a position less exposed to hot sunshine, and in a moisture-retaining soil, but one which drains freely in winter. When preparing the soil for planting well rotted compost and grit should be added. In subsequent years on thin soils additional leafy soil may be

Thymus x *citriodorus* Pers.
Family LABIATAE

worked in amongst the lower stems in the spring. This encourages further rooting and therefore the plants will be more robust. After flowering the current year's growth should be trimmed as suggested for common thyme. This will help to keep the growth of this straggling plant more compact. The more vigorous silver and variegated forms of lemon thyme are ornamental, but far less aromatic.

Culinary Use Lemon thyme may be used on its own or in herb mixtures in any savoury dish and may be added to salads, sauces or stuffings. Many prefer the more subtle and fruity flavour of this thyme to that of the pungent common or black thyme.

Caraway thyme, *Thymus herba-barona*, does not always survive the cold winters of climates cooler than that of its native Corsica. It makes thin wiry shoots which are almost prostrate and as the tips of these make a mat of growth by rooting into the soil it needs a very open and loose soil to encourage this surface rooting. Also, although it needs excellent drainage it must not be allowed to dry out in summer. The darker, rose pink flowers appear later than those of lemon thyme. Its strong and unusual flavour appeals to those who like aniseed. It is recommended as a seasoning for beef and is known as the baron of beef thyme. It adds an interesting flavour to sandwich fillings.

136

Wormwood

This is a much branched perennial indigenous to northern Europe and northern Asia, and is commonly found in England and Scotland in coastal regions. It is a weed of waste land and grows in abundance wherever the drainage is good. The base of the plant is almost woody; from this the erect annual branching growth may be 1·25 cm (5 ft) tall. The leaves, 6–10 cm (2–4 in), oval in general outline, are deeply cut into lobes, and the whole plant is covered with a silky greyish-white down. The flowers are large for this genus and resemble yellow balls; they are in loose branching racemes which form large terminal panicles.

Cultivation   This plant is seldom grown in gardens, although in a large garden it makes an effective subject for the back of a border. The attractive silvery specimen is most appreciated if grown in full sun and on well drained soil. It can be readily propagated by cuttings or by root division. It tolerates colder, bleaker conditions better than southernwood, *A. abrotanum*.

Artemisia absinthium L.
Family COMPOSITAE

Uses Leaves and stems are collected from both wild and cultivated plants and dried for use in medicine. The drug obtained is used in various preparations for promoting digestion and treating gastric complaints, but as with certain other drugs it must never be taken during pregnancy. Infusions of wormwood are used as herbal remedies to reduce fevers, to expel intestinal worms, and to act as a general tonic and restorative.

The bitter principle obtained from the plant is used in small amounts as a flavouring in certain wines and spirits, eg, vermouth. It was formerly the basic ingredient of the potent liqueur absinthe, once very popular in France, but its use is now prohibited by law as it was found that if taken in excess it caused chronic poisoning and permanent damage to the nervous system. It has now largely been replaced by extracts from other herbs.

Yarrow

This plant, also known as Milfoil, a common name obviously derived from the specific name, is native to Europe and is found as a weed in all temperate regions. It is one of the commonest of British wild plants. Neglected pastures which have not been under the plough for a number of years often become completely invaded by it. It has creeping underground stems and erect annual stems about 30 cm (1 ft) high. The leaves, oblong to linear in outline, 2–10 cm ($\frac{4}{5}$–4 in) long, are feather-like and cut into narrow and deeply pinnate segments, hence the specific name *millefolium*. Small clusters of leaves varying in size grow at intervals on the upright flower stem. The numerous flower heads are in dense, flat-topped compound clusters, each flower being 7 mm ($\frac{3}{10}$ in) in diameter with five ray florets, in colour off-white or more rarely pink. The plants may be either densely or sparsely hairy, the white woolly hairs giving them a greyish appearance. Yarrow flowers throughout the summer. It is often a troublesome weed in lawns.

Achillea millefolium L.
Family COMPOSITAE

Cultivation   Yarrow will grow on any soil in an open sunny position. It can readily be propagated by division in autumn or spring. Although the flowers of the wild plants are mostly a dingy white a few forms with pale or deep pink flowers have been selected. Among these are 'Cerise Queen', which is pink, and the deep red 'Fire King'. These make useful garden plants which remain in flower from early summer into the autumn.

Uses   The common names of *Achillea*, staunch weed and soldiers' weed, are an indication of the ancient use of the plant. It is said that the legendary Greek warrior Achilles, the hero of the Trojan War, saved the lives of many of his soldiers wounded in battle by the use of this herb. Belief in its efficacy as a healing agent has persisted down the ages, and even to this day the drug is considered to be helpful in arresting internal haemorrhage. It improves the circulation, induces perspiration in feverish conditions and relieves digestive disorders, and is also used in external applications for rashes and in mouth washes for inflamed gums. It is said that an ointment made from yarrow applied to the scalp will arrest hair loss, and the juice can be used as a shampoo.

Yarrow, with other weeds such as nettles and Russian comfrey, *Symphytum × uplandicum*, is a valuable activator when added to the compost heap.

Further Reading

Books giving recipes for the culinary use of herbs are followed by the letter (C), and those giving information about medicinal use of herbs are followed by the letter (M).

Arber, Agnes, *Herbals, Their Origin and Evolution*, Cambridge University Press, 1938; new ed. 1953.

Brownlow, Margaret, *Herbs and the Fragrant Garden*, Herb Farm, Seal, 1957; 3rd ed, Darton, Longman & Todd, 1978.

Clair, Colin, *Of Herbs and Spices*, Abelard-Schuman, 1961.

Coats, A.M., *Flowers and Their Histories*, Hulton Press, 1956; A. & C. Black, 1968.

Culpeper, Nicholas (1616–64), *Culpeper's Complete Herbal*, reprint, W. Foulsham & Co, 1952.

Gabriel, Ingrid, *Herb Identifier and Handbook*, Sterling, New York, 1975 (distributed in Britain by Ward Lock).

Genders, Roy, *Scented Flora of the World*, Robert Hale, 1977.

Grieve, M., *A Modern Herbal*, 2 vols, Cape, 1931; reprinted 1974; Penguin Books, Harmondsworth, 1976.

Hatfield, Audrey Wynne, *The Pleasures of Herbs*, Museum Press, 1964.

Hemphill, John and Rosemary, *Herbs and Spices*, Summit Books, 1978 (C).

Hemphill, Rosemary, *The Penguin Book of Herbs and Spices*, Penguin Books, Harmondsworth, 1966 (C).

Howarth, Sheila, *Herbs with Everything*, Sphere 1977 (C).

Kreig, Margaret B., *Green Medicine*, Harrap, 1965 (M).

Law, N.G.A. Donald, *A Concise Herbal Encyclopaedia*, Bartholomew, 1973 (M).

Le Strange, Richard, *A History of Herbal Plants*, Angus & Robertson, 1977.

Loewenfeld, Claire, *Herb Gardening*, Faber & Faber, 1964 (C).

Loewenfeld, Claire, and Back, Phillipa, *The Complete Book of Herbs and Spices*, David & Charles, 1974 (C).

Mabey, Richard, *Food for Free*, Collins, 1972.

Page, Mary, and Stearn, William T., *Culinary Herbs; Wisley Handbook 16*, The Royal Horticultural Society, 1974.

Ranson, Florence, *British Herbs*, Penguin Books, 1949.

Rohde, Eleanour, *Herbs and Herb Gardening*, The Medici Society, 1936.

Sanecki, Kay Naylor, *The Complete Book of Herbs*, Macdonald and Jane's, 1974.

Schauenberg, Paul, and Paris, Ferdinand, *A Guide to Medicinal Plants*, Lutterworth Press, 1977 (M).

Smith, Archibald William, revised and enlarged by Stearn, W.T., *A Gardener's Dictionary of Plant Names*, Cassell, 1972.

Starý, František, and Jerásek, Václav, *Herbs, a Concise Guide in Colour*, Hamlyn, 1973 (M).

Stuart, Malcolm (editor), *The Encyclopaedia of Herbs and Herbalism*, Orbis, 1979.

Thomson, William A.R. (editor), *Healing Plants; a Modern Herbal*, Macmillan, 1978 (M).

Thomson, William A.R., and Smith, Elizabeth, *Healing Herbs*, BBC Publications, 1978 (M).

Glossary

active principles   The chemical constituents obtained by chemical analysis in a drug plant.

adpressed   Pressed down or lying flat, as hairs on leaf or stem.

alkaloid   A compound containing nitrogen occurring in plants.

allergy   Sensitivity to a particular substance.

annual   A plant completing its life cycle in one year.

anthelmintic   Used against intestinal worms.

antibiotic   Inhibiting the growth of germs.

apetalous   Without petals.

astringent   Having the power to draw together organic tissues and thus check secretion.

awl shaped   Narrow and sharp pointed.

axil   The angle between leaf and stem.

biennial   A plant completing its life cycle in two years.

bitter principles   The chemical constituents of plants, responsible for the bitter taste.

capsule   A dry fruit with more than one carpel.

carminative   Having the effect of expelling flatulence.

compound leaf   A leaf with two or more separate leaflets.

corolla   The whorl of petals in a flower, which may be either separate or joined.

corymb   Flower stems starting from different points but forming a cluster of flowers, the outer flowers opening first.

crenate   Having shallowly round-toothed leaf margins.

cyme   A more or less flat-topped cluster of flowers, with the central flower opening first.

decussate   Of opposite leaves on a stem, each alternating pair at right angles to the preceding pair.

dioecious   Having male and female flowers on different plants.

essential oil   Volatile oil obtained from plants.

febrifuge   Reducing fevers.

glabrous   Without hairs.
glaucous   Leaves with a blue-grey bloom.
glycoside   A substance occurring in plants in which a sugar is combined with another organic compound.

HA   Hardy annual.
hastate   Shaped like an arrowhead, with lobes pointing sideways.
HHA   Half hardy annual, ie, needing to be germinated in a frost-free place.

inflorescence   A flowering branch.
in situ   Of seeds, sown where they are to grow, without transplanting.

linear   With leaves long and narrow, four or five times as long as broad.

metabolism   The chemical processes of growth in plant cells.
mucilage   A viscous substance occurring in certain plants.

oblong leaf   A leaf that is twice or three times as long as broad, margins almost parallel in middle.

orbicular leaf   A leaf that is almost rounded.
organic acid   An acid occurring within a plant.
ovate leaf   A leaf that is scarcely twice as long as broad and wider below the middle.

palmate leaf   A leaf with several veins or lobes diverging from the same point.
pedicel   The stem of one flower in a cluster.
peltate   Peltate leaves have the stalk joined to the under surface of the blade, generally near to the middle instead of near the lower edge.
perennial   A plant which will seed and live for several or many years.
petiole   Leaf stalk.

pinnate A compound leaf with leaflets arranged along either side of a common stalk.

pistil The female or seed-bearing part of a flower, comprising ovary, style and stigma.

pubescent Covered with short hairs.

raceme An inflorescence with flowers borne on pedicels along a single stem.

radical Growing directly from rhizome or root.

receptacle The enlarged extremity of the flower stem to which all or some parts of the flower are attached.

revolute The margins of leaves rolled towards the lower side.

rhizome A root-like stem with buds and feeding roots.

sagittate Shaped like an arrowhead, with basal lobes pointing downwards.

saponin A glycoside in plant tissue causing water to lather.

scape A leafless stem with one or many flowers.

scarious Dry (not green), a thin skin or membrane.

scorpioid Describing the undeveloped flower spike which is coiled like the tail of a scorpion.

sessile Leaves or flowers without stalks.

spathe The bract or leaf surrounding a flower cluster.

spike Sessile flowers carried on an elongated stem.

stigma The part of the pistil that receives the pollen.

stolon An underground stem or sucker which gives rise to a plant or tuber at its tip.

style The more or less elongated part of the pistil, between ovary and stigma.

styptic Having the power to control bleeding by contracting tissues.

tomentose Densely covered with short hairs.

tuber A thickened fleshy root.

unisexual Flowers or plants of one sex only.

Plan for a Decorative Herb Border

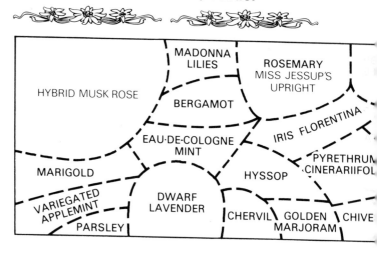

Plan for a Utility Herb Border

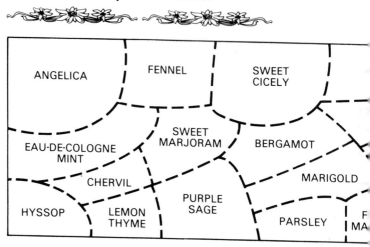

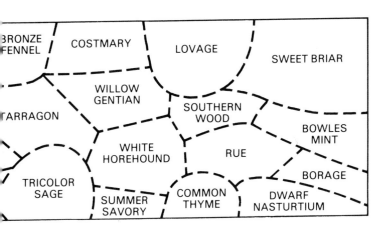

BRONZE FENNEL
COSTMARY
LOVAGE
SWEET BRIAR
TARRAGON
WILLOW GENTIAN
SOUTHERN WOOD
BOWLES MINT
WHITE HOREHOUND
RUE
BORAGE
TRICOLOR SAGE
SUMMER SAVORY
COMMON THYME
DWARF NASTURTIUM

0 _____ 1·5 metres
0 _____ 5 feet

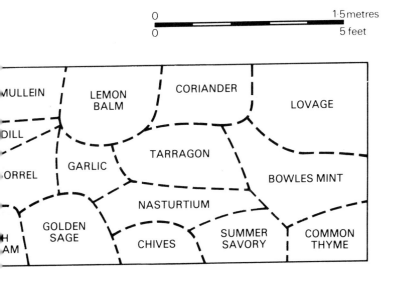

MULLEIN
LEMON BALM
CORIANDER
LOVAGE
DILL
GARLIC
TARRAGON
BOWLES MINT
ORREL
GOLDEN SAGE
NASTURTIUM
CHIVES
SUMMER SAVORY
COMMON THYME

Index

Classifications in this index follow the style used throughout the book. Thus, a family name is printed in capitals and small capitals (e.g. LABIATAE), the generic and specific names in italics (eg, *Achillea millefolium*), and a popular or common name in roman type (eg, agrimony).